SHAOLIN K
The Los

"Developing the Inner Strength"
(Iron Shirt Qi-Gong)

Including the Shaolin Soft Art
TAI-CHI

Peter Love

Includes moves from the Famous Shaolin
Tiger-Crane form the "Sum Chien"
& The "White Crane" form "The Shuang Yang Pei Ho".

Disclaimer.

The author accepts no liability for any injury caused while attempting any of the exercises or techniques described in this book. The words and phrases used, are his own interpretation of those of his master or teachers. At this point the author would like to point out that serious students who wish to practice the art should seek to find a teacher who is willing to teach them. Remember that many masters will not reveal the teachings to students in the early part of their training and will only be taught after the student has shown dedication and loyalty to the master.

Some exercises may prove to difficult for some and therefore a medical expert should be consulted before engaging in any physical exercise.

- All information contained in this book including its photographs, are intended for the use of the purchaser only.

- No reproduction or photocopying is allowed of any part of this book. Without the written permission of the author's legal representative or the author himself.

Published 2007 by arima publishing

www.arimapublishing.com

ISBN 978-1-84549-177-2

Printed and bound in the United Kingdom

Typeset in Palatino

arima publishing
ASK House, Northgate Avenue
Bury St Edmunds, Suffolk IP32 6BB
t: (+44) 01284 700321

www.arimapublishing.com

All proceeds from the sale of this book will help me to continue researching this fascinating martial art and way of life. So that others may then benefit.

Photo front cover: Peter Love demonstrates the bending of a spear.
Back cover: Peter Love demonstrates washing in broken glass.

This book is dedicated to my parents. Without whose help and support over the years during my training, writing this book would not have been possible. Words can never be enough in order to thank you for your help and support.

I hope you enjoy reading the contents of this book.

Love you always.

Peter

A student's reference guide.

The training of any serious martial art will include the co-ordination of the mind (concentration / spirit), body (including arms and legs) and the breath. It is important therefore to break down and practice individual ingredients of the art. Therefore I suggest that you read the book fully before starting any training you may wish to do. As I may mention, something in one section that you will have to read about in another. For example when explaining the soft qi-gong exercises I refer to abdominal breathing, which I explain later under the breathing section.

Once you have read the book you can then use it as a reference guide as it is intended to be. In particular to those training the "Shuang Yang Pei Ho or the "Sum Chien" form/s.

I am sure that on some occasions in the book I may repeat a certain ingredient or subject. One such matter would be that before seriously starting to practice any martial art, you should find a good teacher with a good lineage. If you are unsure about your health consult your doctor first.

Note

I would like to point out that in most cases in this book I have used the word him or he but in many cases could have been written her or she. This is merely to avoid unnecessary use of text during the writing of the book.

Patience!

Practice

Loyalty

Endurance

Time

Patience!

Dedication

Perseverance

Respect

Patience!

"Both teacher and pupil must have patience"

"Prepare yourself for the long journey that lies ahead"

Thank you

My thanks to the Shaolin Master, from Singapore with whom I became a disciple student and to all the Shaolin Masters, both past and present.

My respects to all of my previous instructors, regardless of how little or how much I may have learned from you, some of whom I may have mentioned in this book. Your combined knowledge has allowed me to develop my martial art skills further.

I take this opportunity of thanking those of you who have kindly purchased this book.

Also I would like to thank the publishers for printing what I hope many will find of benefit in their pursuit of excellence in the martial arts and a better way of life.

Finally thanks to my students who have assisted me in the production of this book.

About the Author

Peter Love was born during the Chinese Year of the Rat, in Staffordshire 1961. He as spent most of his life (since the age of nine) studying martial arts and hopes that by writing this book he will encourage others to change their way of life and thinking regarding the training of any martial art.

Trying to put in to words the history of my martial arts training would itself probably require writing a book on its own. I do not believe that there is any person who as studied martial arts or in fact any other subject for any length of time could indeed write a complete book on that subject. I have therefore chosen a small part of the art, which I personally consider the most important.

I first began practicing martial arts in the early seventies while still in primary school. A school friend asked me if I would join the local Karate club. At the time I was a keen footballer and to be fair did not really know what I was going to be doing when I joined. The Karate club was on the first floor and entering via the steps for the first time did get the nerves going a little. However once we had joined and settled in, everything was great and I really enjoyed my training there. This art I eventually began teach to other children before leaving school at sixteen and start my working life. The style I studied was Shukokai Karate and one of the many forms I was taught was *Sanchin*. It was a tension form *(Kata)* that helped to develop the body and power of techniques. I would like to thank my instructors with whom I first began learning the art of Karate.

After about six months or so and a change of employment, I began to study Tae-Kwon-Do a Korean art which introduced me to more competitions and I spent only a few years training before reaching 2nd kup.

In 1979 I began to study Lau Gar kung Fu where I became both a successful instructor and competition fighter. The mid 1980's Lau Gar Team where well known across the country for their continued success in competitions. Thank you to Sifu G. Shaw for his coaching skills particularly regarding competition fighting.

During my training I have also studied various other arts including Shotokan, Shotokai, Jeet-Kune-Do and Kali and freestyle martial arts. By training the different arts it as given me a broad knowledge of the Japanese, Korean and the Chinese martial arts.

After a serious car accident in 1997 I was unable to practice any form of martial art or physical exercise for over six months and when I finally was able to begin my training again I had continuing problems with my back. While this for many would have been enough to give up such a physical activity, I became more determined to train the martial arts. In 1998 I began Shotokai Karate. It was my intention to see if I could still train at a high level. The club only had a few members when I joined and within just a few weeks I was graded based on the forms I had managed to learn. I was immediately upgraded and six months later upgraded to 1st kyu. I continued to practice for the next twelve months then attempted my 1st Dan, which I successfully passed. I then knew that I was able to reach a high level in the art again even with my back problems.

Looking for ways to recover from my accident and with already experience in Chinese martial arts, I began to research more into Chinese Medicine and in particular Chinese Qi-Gong (Chi-Kung).

After years of research and study of various martial arts I joined a Singapore based Shaolin School. After only a few months study I became an instructor although still learning and practicing myself. At this time I was already a full time martial arts instructor at my own centre based in Stoke-on-Trent and this was seen as an addition to the teaching at the centre.

In 2001 I began teaching Southern Shaolin Tiger-Crane Art for the Shaolin, school. Shortly after this I was invited to meet and train with a Shaolin Master from Singapore. In late March 2002 I travelled to Singapore to meet and train with the Master. During this visit I was also privileged to meet another Master of the Lohan & Monkey style as well as the *"iron-shirt"*. While in Singapore I was initiated to train the Shaolin inner-strength known as *"iron shirt chi-kung"*.

After returning to England I was able to meet the Master again on a number of occasions. In the summer of 2002 and 2003 he stayed at my home with my parents during which time he gave seminars to some of my own students. During his first visit he accepted me as one of his Shaolin disciples. A great privilege, as I became one of only a handful of students ever to be initiated by the Master at that time.

I continued to develop my kung fu skills and practised diligently in order to later become both Instructor and grading examiner for the Shaolin group teaching both the combined Tiger Crane Art and the iron shirt.

During my time with this group I performed at various public exhibitions including: London's own celebrations of the Chinese New Year and Autumn festivals that took place at Trafalgar Square and also London's China Town off Leicester Square. I also took part at the SENI 2003 and 2004 exhibitions held at the NEC Birmingham, as well as appearing on the TV *"This Morning"* program, when several of my own students joined myself and other performers to celebrate the Chinese New Year.

In 2004 I left the Shaolin group and unfortunately have not been in contact with my master since. I would however like to point out that leaving this Shaolin school was a decision made by all of my students at that time and not mine alone. As far has I am concerned there were never any problems and still is no grievance between the Master and myself.

I now continue to practice and teach the Shaolin art, along with my students. We still continue to pay our respects to the Master, of whom a photograph remains on the wall at the centre at which I continue to train. He will always remain as one of my teachers who I will always remember and will welcome the master at any time.

I remain dedicated to teaching the original art and aim to preserve the original training methods of the Shaolin Masters.

My centre continues to attract a wide variety of students from beginner to experienced martial artists.

Contents

Introduction

I believe that there is no such thing as a complete guide or book of any martial art or probably even any subject, available today. If there were then the text itself would have to be so small you would not be able to read it! Or indeed the book would need to be so large that you were unable to carry it. Over the years therefore many hundreds of books have been published in order to preserve a certain part off each style or art. This is such a book and its main purpose is to save and record two forms in particular and give the basics of the training required to develop and improve the student.

This book as not been written for personal gain, as this would not be in the true tradition of Shaolin. I do not claim to be a master of *this or of that* style. I consider myself a dedicated practitioner of the art, who is privileged to teach what I know.

The book is designed to open the minds of those that have chosen to read it. It is hoped that regardless of level attained you will find something new that may not have been included in previous books. The book should prove a valuable addition to any serious student of both Kung Fu or the many styles of Karate or even for those who are merely seeking information regarding the martial arts.

Its main purpose is to record the movements of the famous Shaolin *(Sil Lum)* form the "The Sum Chien". I believe that no book offers a full and accurate description, of the art passed down from the masters. As each masters art will vary and the interpretation will inevitably change over the years. Although one thing is certain, all the great masters will insist on their students practicing the Sum Chien form on a daily basis, confirming that the practice of the basics is the way to mastering the Shaolin art!

Many people consider martial arts as a hobby and will practice their chosen art for one or two hours each week. Some practice more especially those who wish to compete in competitions etc. This does not however represent a true art.

However for those who wish to develop their art to the highest level then their Kung Fu or chosen art becomes a way of life!

It would be fair to say that I am unable to put in to a single book the entire Shaolin art, its principles, training methods, techniques and theories etc.

The book however I hope will encourage you to pursue your chosen art with a renewed interest. Should you wish to train in any martial art, then seeking a good teacher/instructor should be the first thing that you do. Check how long the instructor has trained and choosing one who began his training before the Bruce Lee era would be well recommended.

Although Bruce Lee did grab the attention of the western world he unfortunately introduced the *"cowboy"* instructor. Shortly after his fame, both the mid and late seventies turned some *"novice"* martial artists with less than two years training regardless of style, into *kung fu "masters"* overnight. Sadly those instructors went on to teach others and the quality of instruction for the following generations was very weak to say the least.

Research the various styles before choosing which one to practice. Choosing the Shaolin art will generally mean that you have found the original art and therefore you will have the chance to train the many styles which are now taught separately by the more modern arts.

You will not learn Shaolin kung fu in a kickboxing class and beware of instructors who try to impress you with a show of trophies. Any one who tells you that you can master the art in a few years, are clearly not studying Shaolin kung fu. Avoid schools that teach you how to do press-ups, sit-ups and loads of physical exercise. Although physical fitness is important, spending half, or even more of your class time on this type of workout suggests that you will not be learning much kung fu.

There is so much to study that every lesson you attend you will feel that there is something new to practice or to improve upon. I do not mean just new forms when I say learn something new.

It would be normal for new beginners to attend classes once or twice each week. As most classes are for about one hour, further practice should be done at home. Your instructor will notice the improvement and it will also show him that you are dedicated to learning.

Once you have settled with your new school and have completed your preparation course. Your training schedule will increase and you should look to attend more classes each week possibly three or four.

As I mentioned earlier if you wish to seriously study the art then it no longer becomes a hobby but a way of life! It would not be a normal day if I personally did not practice qi-gong or kung fu during some part of the day.

A typical day for myself, would involve the practice of soft qi-gong, either done standing or moving. The Shuang Yang *(tai chi)* would then be practiced followed by several sets of Da Mo and hard qi-gong. The day continues with the practice of the traditional forms and would include the use of weapons. After a period of further relaxation and meditation my day will draw to an end. At which point my mind and body are relaxed and ready for the next day. I do not practice everything every day, as this would not be possible. There are simply not enough hours in the day. I carefully select what I want to practice from each part of the art and spend quality time on improving what I am already doing.

There are many martial arts books available today plus videos and of course now the dvd. You can learn new skills from such sources but will need a teacher to guide you through your learning in the early years of study. Do not think that you do not need to learn anymore because you have achieved a high-ranking grade. This is just the start of your martial arts training. After over thirty-six years of training I still try to develop my skills in order to improve my life further.

A Brief History of Southern Shaolin
from the *Fukien* District

Many martial arts trace their roots back to one of a number of Shaolin temples in China. The art to which we are paying particular attention can be traced back to the famous Southern Shaolin Temple in the *Fukien (fujian)* district. The Southern Styles tend to train and concentrate on firm stances, hand techniques and low range kicks. But include the use of high crane style kicks, throwing and ground fighting techniques.

Much of the Shaolin art is traced back to the teachings of the Indian monk Da Mo *(Tamo) (Bodhidarma)*.

It is said that Da Mo left India and travelled to China to teach Buddhism. *(I have not included any guide to Buddhism in this book. There are many books available on this subject and the teachings vary from country to country).*

His journey began possibly as early as 497 A.D. On arrival at the Shaolin temple he discovered that the monks were both weak and sickly. He therefore retired to a cave and meditated for nine years during which time he had devised a set of exercises that would eventually improve the monks physical condition and once incorporated into their Kung Fu training increase the effectiveness of their martial arts. The exercises taught by Da Mo became so popular that they now form the basis of any Shaolin art practiced today.

In the mid 17th century the Southern Temple became famous for producing some of the best fighters, and many rebels who were opposed to the foreign rule at that time, came to the *Fukien* temple to perfect their fighting skills. The Manchurian government knew that the opposition was gathering pace and that the *Fukien* temple posed a great threat to them. The Manchurian government decided that they would send an army in order to defeat the opposition. But rather than fighting face to face they decided to set fire to the temple killing many inside at the time. Many of the southern fighters were either killed during the fire or killed during their escape by the surrounding army. However it is said that five Kung Fu masters managed to escape both the fire and the surrounding army and once they had found safety decided to split up and continue to travel through China. Wherever they went they would gather new groups of people who were prepared to fight in order to defeat the foreign government. Many secret societies were set up throughout China and eventually the Manchurian rule was finally defeated.

During the Chinese revolution many of the top Kung Fu master's fled the country and emigrated to the nearby islands of Singapore, Malaysia, Indonesia the Philippines and Hong Kong where they continued to teach the original art.

Why Study Kung Fu?

In today's world most people practice kung fu because their parents and friends want them to learn self-defence. Although this is great for the person who is learning, it is important that the student wants to learn also. It is very difficult to teach someone who does not want to be there!

Q. Do you want to learn Shaolin Kung Fu?
Q. Do you want to fight all of the time?
Q. Do you want or need to get fit / healthier?
Q. Do you want to learn how to defend yourself?
Q. Do you want to enter tournaments and perform?
Q. Do you want to learn a traditional art?

Ask yourself the above questions before joining a new club. Most people will want one or two of the items listed above.

If you wish to engage in fighting all of the time then traditional schools are probably not the best as most time should be on learning the art and therefore actual fighting time should be much less than say a modern kickboxing class, where the student can expect to fight for most of the lesson.

However if you spend hours doing physical workouts and punching and kicking bags you need to ask the question what am I learning? Are you being taught how to punch and kick correctly? Are you able to withstand an attack of a similar nature or have you developed little defensive skills?

So you only want to get fit and be healthier.

Well many and including your doctor would probably suggest that you started walking or jogging it's much cheaper than going to a gym or any martial art club. But many people turn to martial arts because there is much more to do.

You want to learn how to defend yourself?

What do you want to defend yourself against? Empty-hand techniques? Weapons?

The art of self-defence against any attack would be to avoid the attack in the first place. To successfully defend against any attack cannot and should not be guaranteed by any instructor. If you have to defend yourself, in particular against a blade attack, then it is almost certainly going to mean someone getting injured or even killed. To defend against such an attack takes years of practice and all the great masters will say, "expect to get cut" when defending against a blade attack. If however this is what you want to study then traditional clubs should teach you the correct method of disarming an attacker. Beginners would not however normally learn such skills. A student's attitude would play an important part on what and when they were taught certain skills.

Should you want to enter tournaments or perform at exhibitions or similar.

Traditional clubs, who teach tournament fighting and forms would enable you to have an opportunity to enter either as a fighter or performer or both if you so desire. The kickboxing clubs should have access to tournament fighting.

So you want to learn a traditional art?

This will involve learning basic stances, blocks, punches, kicks etc plus traditional forms and should offer the opportunity of learning how to use the many weapons available. Beware however some clubs do not always teach weapons and once again it would be unusual to teach beginners how to use weapons.

You want to learn Shaolin Kung Fu?

A Shaolin school should teach you all the ingredients to develop your martial art skills. You should have the opportunity of performing if you wish to do so. I would however like to point out that Shaolin fighting skills are not used in modern competition fighting. It would not be possible for the experienced fighter to use the skills and techniques they have learned against a single opponent. Clearly this would mean the opponent being seriously injured or even killed. The art is therefore watered down so as to allow students to practice or enter tournaments. Once you begin sparring with a partner or an opponent during competition you are no longer practicing the true Shaolin art of fighting.

Learning Shaolin Kung Fu will involve hard work. It will mean dedication, perseverance, loyalty, respect and much more.

"A way of life not just a martial art"

A Shaolin school will become your second home and you should always feel welcome when you are there. You should avoid alcohol and drugs at all times. This is a way of life not just a martial art.

Now read the book and then decide if you wish to be part of the amazing Shaolin Brotherhood!

Warming Up and Stretching

It is essential that you should undergo a thorough warm up before practicing any martial art or in deed any sport or exercise. Most Shaolin arts will teach the student how to warm up without causing any serious injury.

Many will teach soft *qi-gong* exercises during the early stages of your training. You can also expect to learn hard qi-gong and the Da Mo exercises which are all part of the Shaolin daily training routine.

The soft qi-gong is normally an exercise that is practiced during the early morning. While the hard qi gong exercises would normally precede the practice of the Shaolin forms.

Typical warming up exercises would include jogging or running, the rotating of the arms forwards backwards and to the sides. Stretching the body forwards sideways and backwards etc. The rotating of the shoulders, elbows, wrists, hips, knees and ankles and the general stretching of both the arms and legs.

The stretching is important and your body must be warm in order for you to be able to stretch safely without causing injury. This will help with the flow of qi and the blood circulation. You should remain relaxed when stretching and do not force the stretch beyond the body's capability. This will only cause pain and injury.

It is important to loosen the body as well as the limbs.

You may choose to engage in more physical exercise such as sit-ups, press ups squat thrusts etc. It is however not essential as the forms alone are exercise enough. The cat stretch is an excellent exercise when done correctly!

Start slowly and increase the speed as you warm up. Once thoroughly warm begin your hard qi-gong and Da Mo exercises then practice your kung fu techniques and routines. This may include the use of Shaolin weapons and or partner routines.

The body can be resembled to a rubber band. When in regular use it stays supple. But when not used it will become brittle and eventually snap when stretched.

The Shaolin forms include all the exercises to stretch and develop the body both physically and mentally.

However many of the exercises are not seen by simply watching the form. This is why many of the modern arts are only visually copying the original art but are in fact not actually doing it!

Cooling Down

Just as you have warmed up to enable you to practice. It is equally as important to cool down in a similar manner.

Cool downs generally consist of the same warm up exercises but done much slower with an obvious emphasis on relaxing and cooling down. Therefore no physical exercises would be necessary. Taking a shower after training will help relax the muscles after their physical workout.

A few minutes simple meditation practice would also be of great benefit to help calm the mind. Students will need to calm down much more before leaving the club, especially after sparring sessions.

The soft qi-gong exercise of slapping the body, which is explained later, is often used at the end of a cool down session and with a few minutes meditation.

Theory

Without a theory the art would not exist.

The Southern Crane style when first practiced by the beginner will feel hard and developing the subtleness of the crane can feel like a lifetime away. This is because generally in today's world most people think fighting requires brute force and it is usual for students to be very stiff or tense. The mention of becoming soft, flexible and supple can be seen as a weakness to many. Only when you have practiced the art for several years do you begin to realize the benefits of training to develop the softness can be more useful than you could have ever imagined.

When first starting it is natural to be hard and during this period the muscles will no doubt, become much stronger.

However, once you become softer you will increase your skills in the art of sticking to an opponent, therefore, allowing you to take control of the opponent and as an opening arises you can strike to the unprotected areas. Normally the vital areas of eyes or groin are typical attacking points of the crane style.

When first starting, learn and develop the hard qi-gong exercises in order to increase your strength. The practice of the Shaolin empty hand form known as the "Sum Chien" will develop the body both physically and mentally. After which time the development of the tiger-crane forms will train you to become softer in your actions but you will find that your techniques, either defence or attack will feel much stronger. Resulting in lightening fast penetrative strikes that your attacker will not see, but in fact, only feel!

"The training of Kung Fu is based on achieving perfection. If we remember that no one is perfect then improving on what we have learned so far will always be possible"

The Dan Tian (Tan Tien)

I will refer to the *dan tian (tan tien)* on several occasions and therefore for reference will briefly explain where they are. There are a number of dan tians that would be referred to as chakra's when practicing yoga. I will however only refer to the ones that are commonly used regarding our training.

- **High level** *dan tian,* is positioned at the centre between the eyes.

- **Middle level** *dan tian,* is positioned at the solar plexus.

- **Lower level** *dan tian,* which is often mentioned, is situated about one and a half inches to two inches below the navel.

The lower level is considered to be the main energy centre for the body and great emphasis is placed on breathing from this point. Sink your energy to your lower *dan tian* and store it for later use. It is important to your kung fu training to build up the amount of qi stored in the lower dan-tian. This is why many Shaolin practitioners remain in the horse stance for long periods of time. It contributes to building the level of qi in the dan-tian.

The *dan tians* play an important part in your balance when stepping or standing on one leg. Better balance will be achieved if your *dan tians* are all in a straight line with your heel.

Your lower dan tian will be the receiver of external qi and the training of the mind will allow you to distribute it to any part of the body.

Other dan tians would be at the top of the head and various points of the spine. This is why it is important to keep the spine straight when practicing qi-gong.

The most often used breathing pattern in qi gong exercises is that of dan-tian breathing. The diaphragm moves downward as the lower abdomen moves forward during the inhale phase. During the exhale phase the diaphragm lifts and the abdomen contracts towards the center of the body. The breath is drawn into the body through the nose and may be exhaled through either the nose or mouth depending upon the exercise being performed.

Qi (Chi)

In general terms *qi* can be described as energy or air and is therefore within and all around us.

Like many of the aspects of martial arts training this section itself could fill a book of its own.

It is our aim to improve our breathing so that our bodies function correctly. It is therefore important then when practicing qi-gong we breathe in as much fresh air as possible. This is why we often take our students on training camps near fresh coastal areas where the air is much fresher. It is important that we do not abuse our bodies with drugs or alcohol, as this will affect the qi both inside and around us.

We should therefore try to live as healthy life style as possible in order to improve our own energy fields and the energy around us.

The basic soft qi-gong exercises shown in this book are not designed to cause injury to anyone who chooses to practice them. They are clearly an exercise routine to help prevent illness. They will help unite Heaven, Earth and Human qi. The exercises will involve the visualization of drawing on both the Heaven and Earth's qi and balance it with our own.

It would however be advisable to seek guidance from your teacher who will help correct your movements and develop the exercises for you.

The Chinese have studied qi-gong like kung fu for thousands of years. It is now well known that many qi-gong practitioners live a healthy and long life and many masters have extended their lifestyle well past one hundred.

When practicing the soft qi-gong exercises maintain a good posture. Concentrate on rooting and your balance. Your breathing should be slow, calm and be in time with each movement.

Empty your mind and relax the body. Do not overstretch but allow the body to find its own level.

The practice of qi-gong is an important part of Shaolin training. Do not pass it by or you will fail to develop the art further.

To master some of the qi gong exercises will involve giving up any sexual activity. This will allow you to build up the vital energy required for your training. This is why very few people probably ever learn and are able to master the art, as for many giving up what is a part of everyday life is not always possible. Any student in a sexual relationship will probably find some of the training not possible. It does not mean that you may never engage in a sexual relationship ever again. It is the early part of some of the training that will require you not to participate in such acts. This can be up to one hundred days some times may require more and for some less.

Qi-gong
(Soft)

The practice of qi-gong stimulates the body's energy levels through gentle and slow exercises. These subtle but effective exercises activate the circulation of blood and the flow of qi *(energy)* along the meridians. It involves the use of the mind when after regular practice the student can guide their qi to any part of the body. This may be used to strengthen or heal, in the main it will help to prevent illness.

Qi-gong can be practiced in different ways and can involve simple exercises where the student remains standing in one position. Or it may involve such exercises where the student will make basic steps during each movement. These may include a wide range of stances growing in difficulty as the student progresses. Each Step would be coordinated with the relevant hand movements.

Above and opposite: Students practice the soft qi gong exercises during an early morning session.

It can also involve self-massage a technique that has an important healing role. Research indicates that qi-gong may in fact be helpful in order to reduce blood pressure, strengthen the immune system and over a period of time it appears to improve the heart function. It has been claimed that the practice of qi-gong helps to cure and even prevent serious diseases and extend the human life span beyond the average length. Whilst many doubt this in the west the combination of qi-gong breathing, concentration and gentle exercise has to be beneficial for many stress related illnesses.

Are you able to practice qi-gong?

The answer in many cases should be yes. It is for both male and female students regardless of age or fitness level. Students begin basic qi-gong as young as five and will continue the practice throughout their lives. People can begin practicing even when in there seventies. As long as you do not try to do more than the body is capable, you will see improvement in your breathing and flexibility over a period of time. Women may still practice qi-gong even when pregnant but certain exercises may be withdrawn so as not to harm the unborn baby. It would be advisable not eat for about one hour (times may be less in some cases) before and after the exercise. But equally do not starve yourself before exercise.

Basic Soft Qi-gong Exercises

- The following exercises are ideal for people wishing to begin the practice of qi-gong. Remember to start slowly and work within the body's natural capabilities. That is, do not over stretch,

1. Adopt a standing position similar to the horse stance, begin by taking five to seven abdominal breaths during which time try to relax the whole of the body. Place your hands in front of the lower dan-tian. The left palm should be between the dan-tian and the right palm for the male and opposite for females. The tongue should be placed on the soft pallet.

During the soft qi-gong exercises visualise opening all the pores and the pressure points. As you inhale visualise fresh qi being absorbed into your dan-tian through the meridians pressure points and pores. When you exhale visualise diseased qi being flushed out of the body via the pores and the soles of your feet.
Repeat the exercise 7 times.

2. Following the above exercise continue by raising your hands upwards from both sides of the body. Once you reach shoulder height, turn the palms upwards continuing the movement until the hands reach above the head with the fingertips facing upwards. Move the hands down towards the top of the head and continue to move them downward along the centre line of your body until reaching the lower dan-tian level. In general breathe in as the arms are raised and breathe out as the arms are lowered

Repeat the exercise 7 times.

3. Begin the third exercise by bringing both hands to the side of your body. Looking at the fingers at all times push the right hand behind and bring it out to the side and in front of you. Continue in a circular motion around to the left side behind and over the head finally returning to the front and back to the waist. The palms should be kept facing up throughout the exercise. The body bends forwards at first and then backwards as the arm passes over the head.

Repeat the exercise 7 times on both sides.

4. Continuing from the third exercise. The hands gather energy by swinging out to the side and forward during which point the body bends forward. Once stretched out the hands are drawn inwards to the upper dan-tian. Continue the exercise by allowing the body to relax and bend backwards the hands drop to the side and the move is then repeated but when drawing the hands in concentrate on the middle dan-tien. The exercise is repeated for a third time this time drawing the hands in to the lower dan-tien. Remember to start with the upper dan-tian and work down then repeat starting from the lower dan-tien and work upwards.

Repeat the exercise 7 times each dan-tien ie 21 times.

5. After completing the fifth exercise lower your hands towards the floor in front of you bending the body forward remaining in a relaxed position. Raise the hands upwards and over the head relaxing and bending the body backwards.

Repeat the exercise 7 times.

6. Following on from the above exercise, place both hands on the knees. Turn your body to the left as you turn bend the right leg and straighten the left. Repeat on the other side.

Repeat the exercise 7 times each side.

7. Relax and stand with the feet about shoulder width apart. Raise the body upwards standing on the ball of the feet. Allow the body to drop and visualise diseased qi being flushed from the body via the 'yong chuen' bubbling well.

Repeat the exercise for as long as necessary but normally 2 to 3 minutes.

8. Cupping the hands to form a hollow pocket begin to slap the body gentle at first. Start with the head then the arms then work down the font of the body from the chest down to the toes continue with each side of the body, inside the legs and the back and back of the legs.

Repeat each exercise 3 times.
This exercise is commonly used during cooling down exercises when practicing the Kung Fu.

9. Raise your hands from the sides and repeat exercise two on reaching the dan-tian allow the body to relax forward moving the hands under the body and then continue the movement along the inside of the legs down towards the toes and up the outside of the legs to hip level, drawing in towards the lower dan-tian.

Repeat the exercise 7 times.

10. While the hands are in front of the lower dan-tian begin to make small circles in a clockwise direction for males and anti-clockwise for females. Perform eighteen circles keeping the palms in front of each other at all times the circles should grow in size and visualize gathering energy with each circle. Once you have completed eighteen circles begin to reduce the size of the circle for a further eighteen times visualize the energy being stored in the lower dan-tian.

11. To conclude the soft qi-gong exercise rub the palms of your hands as if you were washing your face. Then using the fingers begin to comb the hair massaging the side and back of the head.
Repeat the exercise 7 times.

After the above exercises finish with a period of standing meditation for about two to three minutes. During this period of time concentrate on your breathing. When you breathe in, visualize fresh qi (chi) energy entering the body and when you breathe out visualize the body expelling the diseased qi.

Your body should feel warm with your aura increasing with practice. That is, you should feel that an energy field surrounds your body. In actual fact you have. The energy is around us all, otherwise we would not be alive today. Take the energy around you and replenish your body with fresh energy every day.

Once you have increased your energy levels you can learn to control it and redirect it in order to protect or prevent illness.

"Start the day with a Qi-Gong facial massage"

A qi-gong facial massage is well worth the little extra time needed to complete it. It is best performed before starting your day. It would be similar to washing the face, head and neck with water. Each pressure point would receive a gentle massage and stimulation during such an exercise.

"Focus on the now and not the past or future"

In today's busy world, much of our time can be focused on either what has passed us by, or what in fact may lie ahead. We spend time thinking about the day, which has now ended or about something that may have happened last year. We think about tomorrow and what we are going to be doing next month or next year. It is the now we should be thinking about. How relaxed am I? How is my breathing? Take care of the now and the past will be easier to deal with. As for the future what will be will be. But whatever lies ahead we will cope with much better if we concentrate on what is happening now this very minute. Let's improve the "now" and the future for all will be much better.

If while reading this book you spend time relaxing your body you will help ease any aches and pains you may have.

Spend more time concentrating on the depth of your breathing and you will increase your lung capacity. Therefore in the long term improving your health.

Qi-gong
(Hard)

Like the soft qi-gong many training methods exist in the wide variety of Chinese martial arts. The basic training is normally done in the tiger-crane horse stance. *(See stances and postures).* There are many different sets trained by the various styles.

The following are some of the basic hard qi-gong exercises practiced.

1. Standing in the basic horse stance the thumbs are placed on the outer thighs. When you breathe in, relax and as you breathe out grip both your fists. *(Abdominal breathing-beginners) (Reverse breathing can however be used at a later date)*
(Repeat 9 times)

2. With the arms stretched out to the sides and the palms facing upwards breath in and relax as you breathe out visualize holding weights on both hands.
(Repeat 9 times)

3. Lower the hands to the side of the body palms facing in. Breathe in and relax, breath out and push the fingers towards the ground.
(Repeat 9 times)

4. Stretch both hands forwards about shoulder height *(Double dragons go out to sea).* Breathe in and relax, then breath out push the fingers forwards gripping the fingers at the same time.
(Repeat 9 times)

5. With the arms still in the same position as the fourth exercise breathe in and relax and squat keep both feet flat on the floor and keep the back straight. As you breathe out visualize a weight on the

head and begin to stand up pushing the head upwards as if lifting the weight.

(Repeat 9 times)

"Kung Fu is generally described as hard work over a long period of time"

Southern Shaolin Stances and Postures

The following phrases you may here quite often in many martial arts clubs today.

"Why bother with stances and postures?"

"Stances are no longer useful and training old methods don't work anymore!"

"Just find a natural stance that you are comfortable training in!"

"Rooting to the ground will only make you slower!"

"We haven't got time to train stances!"

I could probably go on and fill an entire chapter of quotes from which my students tell me they have been told during previous practice of martial arts.

When you hear something like one of the quotes above it is time to look for a new teacher.

Question. *Why do some instructors fail to teach the basic principles and theories?*

Answer. *They probably have not been taught them in the first place!*

When new students join my centre I tell them they are here to develop themselves to levels they thought were not possible and it will only be achieved if they...

"Practice what failures don't like doing!"

I remember well one instance, when I first told a new student when he first started, that I would not teach him much in the first few months of practice but would give him some basic exercises and stances to work on. At the end of his first lesson he approached and said "Thank you for the lesson you have taught me more in one hour than I have learned over the past six months at my previous club."

"There are no short cuts and the mastering of the basics will allow you to eventually master the art"

Now you are eager to learn more of what many don't even bother with as to the untrained person it appears to be easy or boring!

Start practicing… The essential basics, of the art.

- **Tiger-Crane - Horse Stance**

Front view   *Side view*

Probably the most commonly used stance in all martial arts when training basic techniques. However as I have previously mentioned many modern martial arts fail to include the key ingredients for the stance.

I have therefore taken time to include the basic requirements for this stance.

First adopt a natural shoulder width stance, the shoulder line being inside the heel.

Begin by gripping the floor with each foot. The concentration at this point needs to focus on each foot. The feet should grip like suckers with nine points of each foot in contact with the floor. The nine points are the following five toes, the ball of the foot, the pad, the blade and the heel.

Visualize roots growing from each point of the foot like that of a tree and remember that the way you root now while beginning the exercise will continue to improve each time you practice.

The feet should have a forward facing direction with the toes facing slightly inwards.

The knees should be bent and placed over the centre of the toes.

The hips and chest face forwards and the weight evenly distributed *fifty-fifty* over both left and right sides.

The spine should be in line with the rear heel and the bottom of the spine pressed down towards the ground.

While keeping the spine straight and vertical sink the shoulders downwards.

Raise the chest, the lower dan-tien *(inch and half below the navel)* and testicles.

Keep the head straight and the chin should be tucked in.

Practice the above procedures until you can perform the stance without thinking of the posture.

It is most important that you sink into the stance during your training.

We do not wish to cause injury to anyone training. The stance should however cause some discomfort especially when first starting. If it does not than you are probably not doing it correctly! Bend your legs and sink lower!

The main purpose of this training is to build the strength in the legs and back and develop a good posture for your future training. You do not master this stance by just knowing what to do. You must practice every day and keep developing it.

• Lohan Style - Horse Stance

A variation of the horse stance may also be trained when practicing the *"Lohan"* style.

Open the feet about two shoulders width. Then bend the legs. Keep the same principles as before.

This would be a much lower stance. When in the correct position the top of the legs should be parallel with floor. Try balancing a staff across the legs and remain in the posture for two minutes to begin with. Increase this time during your training. It would be normal for students to practice this stance for up to six months during their preparation level before moving on to the foundation level. Both student and instructor would build their relationship over such a period of time. The posture would be slightly raised once you have developed the strength in the legs. The master may light an incense stick and when it had completely burned the exercise would be complete. Many people give up after as little as twenty or thirty seconds. You must enter a meditative state and ignore what is going on around you. The practice of the stance will build the required levels of qi in the lower dan-tian. This will then allow you to advance later in the art.

- **Walking Stance**

Front view   *Side view*

The walking stance takes on the same principles as the horse stance with the following changes or additions.

- Either the left or right foot is placed one-foot length in front of the other.

- The back foot is facing slightly out and the front foot is facing slightly in, both feet are parallel.

- With the spine in line with the rear heel this increases the weight on the rear foot to about sixty percent.

- The weight from left to right should remain evenly distributed *fifty-fifty*.

All the previously mentioned postures remain the same including the hips and chest facing forward.

- Remember to *sink* your energy into the ground.

- **Bow and Arrow or Forward Stance**

Front view   *Side view*

(Used in the White Crane and the Shaolin Staff Form)

Place either the left or right, foot one and a half foots length in front of the other.

The back foot is facing slightly out and the front foot is facing slightly in, both feet should be parallel. The weight is concentrated more forward but is evenly distributed over left and right side *fifty-fifty*. The centre of the body should therefore remain in a central position and should not finish more over the left or right side.

Keep the hips and chest facing forward during basic practice.

Note. The body will twist to face left or right when executing certain techniques.

- **Cat Stance**

Front view   *Side view*

Start feet together. Turn either left or right foot to face 45 degrees. Place the other foot in front of the rear heel with all the weight on the supporting back leg raise the heel of the front foot so that only the toes are resting on the floor. There should be no weight on the front foot so as to enable you to raise the leg when kicking without moving the body position.

The stance is common when performing the groin kick or the crane kick.

There are many variations of the stances shown in this book when practicing training and additional stances would include "cross stances" "back stances" plus "low and high stances"

The Sum Chien

The Famous Shaolin Empty Hand Form

Many styles over the years have copied the forms performed by the shaolin masters, but only a few were ever taught the inner art itself. Therefore several versions of the form are now being taught. The form may also be known as "Sam Chien" by some styles or by the Japanese name of Sanchin.

The Sum Chien is the first form taught of the combined tiger-crane style. This is because although it looks like a basic set of moves the development of the form through practice has benefits that are not seen by the onlooker but only appreciated by the practitioner. Many masters have trained this form and it was not unusual for them to have to practice it for up to four years before being taught anything else.

The Sum Chien can be translated into 'The three wars' and when you have begun your training in depth you will begin to realise why. Each step will be your own war and only one of which you can decide *victory or defeat*. Start slowly and increase your training concentrating on each individual move. Only after several years training will the practitioner fully appreciate the benefits of the Sum Chien. Cut short your training and you will never understand it. Many master's would say "to master the Sum Chien is to master the art itself." Remember to be patient and train diligently and above anything else you may practice, practice and train the Sum Chien!

The form combines the tiger and crane art. As the Monks watched the tigers in action they observed their strength, courage and power therefore it became a key style to be included in their kung fu training.

The crane performs many circular techniques. It is soft and relaxed and will defeat its opponent with minimum effort. It is evasive but once in contact with its enemy it sticks to it until it finds an opportunity to strike. When it strikes it is with both speed and power. The crane is known for its longevity and great concentration. Anyone who stands on one leg for hours at a time will require great balance and concentration. Combining the two arts together although at first may be difficult for some one it clearly is a successful art.

When training the Shaolin art the emphasis can be placed on the breathing, strength and technical form. By dedicated concentration on these elements your kung fu skills will continue to develop. By combining the *mind, body and spirit* the practitioner can develop their kung fu skills to new heights that they at first thought were impossible.

All the forms are taught at different levels. The ingredients will be added as you develop and what you do at foundation level will change at basic, intermediate and advanced levels. It would be normal to water down the techniques for beginners.

Begin your training with the following exercises:

Many martial artists learn bad habits during their early training. Take a look at some of the high-grade students in many clubs, whose basic fist position can be wrong!

The Sum Chien form teaches the student the correct way of making a fist as well as conditioning the hand. It is like the rest of your kung fu. Such an exercise is so important it remains part of your daily practice for the rest of your life.

- **Exercise 1**

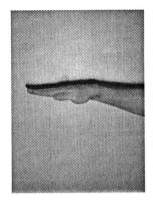 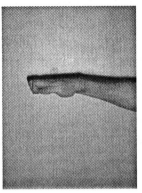 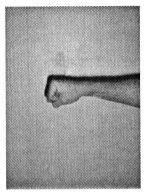

Squeeze the first knuckles of both hands as if beginning to make a fist continue to form a fist shape with both hands, wrapping the thumbs under the centre and across the fingers. Grip as if crushing something in each hand. Relax the grip and point the fingers forward then repeat the exercise 9 times in total.

- **Exercise 2**

Repeat the above exercise then push the elbows inwards and the wrists outwards at the same time. Repeat the exercise 9 Times.

- **Exercise 3**

Now you have begun training the first two exercises I want you to add the sinking of the shoulders - this should be done after exercise 1. Following the gripping of the fists pull the shoulders backwards as if trying to touch each shoulder blade together then try to sink them downwards while in this position continue with exercise 2.

Now you have the basics of the training continue to practice on a daily basis.

Practice times will vary from student to student, but don't be in a hurry as you have a lifetime ahead of you to develop the skills required to master the art.

The Chinese masters developed the ability to relax the body when performing the above exercise and this can be achieved through basic meditation. Many students believe that they have learned to relax when in fact they are still considerably tense.

Kung fu techniques are performed best when the body is relaxed. There is a whip like sound at the end of each technique.

You must now, if not already practicing, learn how to relax. This will ultimately increase your speed and therefore increase your power. Remember that when you think that you have learned how to relax, that you find that you can relax even more!

Stand in an upright position with the feet shoulder width apart.

The weight should be evenly distributed 50/50 over both feet.

Keep both feet firmly on the ground throughout your training.

You should have the feeling that you have roots growing from the feet into the ground and your body should be sinking at all times.

Try to keep the spine straight the base of the spine should be tucked down and the groin should be raised upwards.

Facing forward draw the hands back to the side of the body.

The palms should be facing upward to the sky and the blades of the hands should be resting against the soft points on both sides of the body, which the elbows have passed by.

From this position throw the hands forwards twisting the palm to face downward at the end of the technique.

Keep your elbows in to avoid injury.

When you have completed your technique complete the three previous exercises you have been training regarding the gripping of the fist.

Keep trying to improve your relaxation and soon you will hear the whip like sound on the completion of your technique.

Train slowly at first. This is when you are most likely to get injured. Many will mistake the sound of the joints cracking as the whip like sound. This is, however, not the case.

By repeating this exercise your health, fitness and body toning will all improve.

Hand Positions
(Basic Guide)

In many of the techniques shown the striking or blocking hand will pass through a certain point. That point is known as the soft point. Many Instructors teach you to have your hand placed on the hip. This again would be a misinterpretation of the art. Although a technique can start from any position and in many cases may start even lower than the hip position it would however, in most cases pass by the soft point.

The location can be easily found. Stand in a relaxed position bend the arms and where they touch the side of your body you will find your soft point. It should be just below your ribcage. Make sure your shoulders are relaxed or you may be too high. Now pull your fist or hand back to this point keep the palm facing up. The elbows should be kept in and you should not turn them out as the arm strikes forward. There are a few exceptions but the technique/s would probably not be travelling forward in a straight line.

If you do not pass by the point your techniques are likely to sweep upwards rather than forward. Should you allow the elbows to come away from the body this will seriously weaken your strike and if you twist the wrist too soon you will not have the same effect at the end of your technique.

This soft point of the body releases energy, which is gathered by the hand as it passes by.

Most techniques in Shaolin kung fu will finish with a twist and a gripping motion to ensure each one is a strong, powerful technique. You must learn to relax your body and eventually you will develop a more spring like action to your techniques. Do not be tense when striking but be firm! If your teacher cannot demonstrate the difference then find one who can.

Opening of the Sum Chien

The following information is for guidance only and its main purpose is to record the moves for future generations. It does not include the internal training of the form.

Including the poetic Chinese translations.

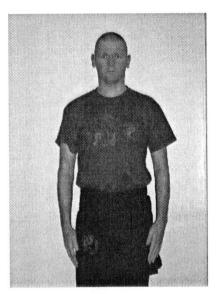

Start from a standing position with the feet together and the hands by the sides.

After first bowing pull both hands to the side of the body with both fists closed. This is the soft point referred to in hand positions

The wrists will face up and the elbows kept in. Step with the right foot into a horse stance.

(The General carrying the seal)

The Sum Chien Form then continues with a traditional Shaolin salute of one hand open and one forming a clenched fist. The left hand is placed under the right clenched fist.

(Brothers across the four seas)

Both hands then move forward in line with the middle dan tien (solar-plexus).

(The displaying of flowers)

After which the hands are opened with the left palm over the centre of the right palm and both facing down. The hands are drawn into the chest and are then turned over and lowered to the lower dan tian position from here the hands are stretched outwards towards each side and the elbows are kept in. This move should create firmness in each arm and the body in general.

(Two pillars piercing the earth)

Once the move has been completed the hands are drawn back to the soft point on the side of the body and with both fists clenched the hands are thrown out in a fast punching like action.

(Beauty looking in the mirror)

Both hands are then opened with fingers facing downwards the hands are thrown in a whip like action into the double upper outer block. Finally both palms twist to face forward and drop so that the fingers are in line the shoulders.

The opening moves should be practiced slowly at first in order to remember each one. Do not cut them short. Increase the speed and power over time. This is the traditional opening of the Sum Chien when practicing the combined Tiger-Crane Art.

(Double dragons going out to sea)

Step forward with the right foot into a Shaolin walking stance as previously explained both hands should be pulled back to the soft point at each side of the body. Once rooted both hands should be thrown in a forward direction as if you were striking the shoulders remember to twist the hand over before the arms lock out, keep the fingers pressed together throughout the movement.

The final position should form a ninety-degree angle across the chest and arms, with both arms parallel with the floor. When performed correctly you will develop a whip like action with each strike.

(Sitting limbs or sinking branches)

Once you have completed the double dragon move, begin the exercise that you have already started to practice. That is, closing the fingers to form a clenched fist then turning the elbows in and pushing the wrists out. This will form the firmness in both arms and body.

Repeat the above exercise 6 times in total stepping forward 3 times and backwards three times so as to finish in a left foot forward stance.

The next set of techniques should be performed with speed and strength with the whip like action.

(The lobster throwing out its pincers)

Step forward into a right stance drawing both hands back to the soft point. Keep both hands clenched throw forward to about chin height and into a wider position than the shoulder width.

(The golden scissors)

Both hands are drawn in together with the left fist behind the right and the forearms pressed together.

(Double scissor hand)

The left hand then blocks/strikes downward with the fingers facing inwards and the technique is then repeated with the right hand.

(Double arrow hand)

The left hand then executes a forward strike in a similar way to that of the double dragon strike and is then repeated with the right hand.

(The child carrying the tablet)

The form is concluded with a shuffling move backwards and finishing in the position shown.

(Two pillars piercing the earth)

Then after returning to the horse stance the *(Two pillars piercing the earth) technique* is performed before finally stepping with the right foot up to the left foot bringing you into the feet together position and both hands drawn to the side where a final bow is made.

The moves of the form are developed and refinement of the form takes place during your training.

It would be normal to practice the Sum Chien form at least three times a day. The movement of the body and the spine play an important role in the development of the form.

"It is better to defend than attack"

"But a defence may in fact be an attack"

A Shaolin practitioner would only ever defend himself against an attacker in circumstances of extreme danger. His defence itself however should become an attacking technique.

Facial Exercises

After training the stances and the techniques of the Sum Chien form for about six months the facial exercises may be added.

While performing the Sum Chien the practitioner should:

- Open the eyes wide and stare in to infinity.

- Open both the nostrils wide

- Pull the ears backwards as if you were trying to hear a whisper from many miles away.

- The sides of the mouth are dropped.

- The teeth are closed together locking the jaw in place.

Do not however, grind the teeth together.

All the above exercises both strengthen and increase the senses. Keep the chin tucked in and the tongue to the soft pallet.

Continue to practice everyday and begin to develop your sixth sense.

Breathing
(The Basics)

Often overlooked by many martial artists, the breathing is most important if you wish to develop the art.

The Sum Chien includes the use of the reverse breath and should be included after about six months practice of the form. Until then concentrate on the stance, posture, relaxation and the techniques. *(See Reverse Breathing).*

Any practice of martial arts should include breathing. The practice of breathing should be done at times other than when practicing the actual martial art techniques. The master's would use Chinese qi-gong exercises in order to improve their breathing so that the various ways of breathing can be developed in such a way that they do not have to think about the way in which they breathe when practicing their kung fu skills.

There are many ways that breathing can be trained. Most practice will include breathing in and out through the nose. In some cases single nostril breathing can be trained. This would be done by closing one nostril with the thumb and breathing in fully with the open nostril and then breathing out through the same nostril. An alternative may be to breathe in through the open nostril, close it using your third finger and breathe out through the other nostril.

Although we continue to increase our depth of breathing, it would be common practice not to breathe to a maximum when training this would result in you likely having to expel air quicker and like wise we would not want to breathe out fully so as not to cause us to gasp for air. When for example you swim under water you are better to take in less than your maximum lung capacity this will help you to hold your breath longer and not get out of breath too soon. It is the same when we practice our forms. Although when we are emitting enormous amounts of energy it is inevitable that we will want to breathe more often and may get out of breath sooner. The more we practice our breathing technique the more we increase our lung capacity and the more energy we can then emit when practicing our techniques.

Abdominal Breathing

Just like a new born baby breathes naturally from birth this is what is known as abdominal breathing. When you breathe in, the stomach expands and when you breathe out it contracts.

Over the years however many people stop breathing in this way and use only half or in some cases even less than their normal lung capacity.

Their stomach would therefore rarely ever expand. If the chest expands they believe they have taken in enough air for each cycle of breath they require. Breathe in slowly and time your period of inhalation. Then time your exhalation. In many cases this would be less than twenty seconds or so. Whatever it is simply concentrating and breathing more slowly and fully will improve it.

When you breathe in the anus is gently pushed out and when you breathe out is gently lifted.

Reverse Breathing

The tongue should be placed on the soft pallet and you should breathe in through your nose. When practicing the reverse breath the abdomen should withdraw as you inhale and expand when you exhale.

A fast exhalation of the breath is required during the "sum chien" training.

When you exhale fast you should make the *"Ha"* sound opening the mouth slightly allowing air to pass either side of the tongue.

There are many exercises in order to develop this type of breathing. Initially as you breathe in practice lifting the dan-tian then as you breathe out throw the dan-tian downwards.

The development of the breathing is an essential part of the Shaolin art. At first it will be trained in a basic format. Ingredients are added over a period of time.

There are of course additional procedures to be carried out when practicing the iron shirt breathing. The diaphragm plays an important part and helps to squeeze and pack the internal organs. The diaphragm is lowered when breathing in and raised when breathing out.

The practice of the reverse breathing will include squeezing and packing the organs, lowering the diaphragm and lifting the perineum *Hui Yin* and include pulling in the anus when breathing in and pushing it out as you breathe out.

The reverse breathing, like the techniques, needs to be developed on its own. So take time to practice the breathing exercises.

Partner Exercises

First breathe in raising the dan-tian at which point your partner should place both hands around the waist and begins squeezing the waist. Once you have completed your inward breath, breathe out fast throwing the dan-tian downwards thus pushing your partner's hands open. This will take a lot of practice in order to develop this technique. Start slowly at first and increase the speed of the outward breath. The continued practice will develop the inner springy-strength used in the Sum Chien form and the Shaolin techniques. Warning, as you begin to develop this technique take care when choosing your partner. The risk of injury mainly that of possibly breaking your partners thumbs are increased. Remember that if you have no partner willing to train with you, you cannot train some of the techniques and exercises described.

As you develop the exercise the training will include breathing to new higher levels. This would include squeezing and packing the dan tian. Many would say that when you can resist the strike of an axe you have begun to master the *springy* art.

Raising the testicles

I thought I would briefly mention the raising of the testicles during the Sum Chien practice, as this exercise for any student studying the martial arts will I am sure raise a question for their instructor the next time they meet.

During the practice of the Sum Chien the student can focus his qi to his genitals and withdraw his testicles upwards and inside the body. Great focus is required and even after many years of practice many students are unable to perform this exercise.

The successful practice of such an exercise will obviously allow the student to withstand strikes to the groin. As well as the important development of the mind, body and spirit.

At this point I think it is safe to say that you can now understand why at first glance the Sum Chien can be easily misunderstood and that the form is in fact an advanced part of the Shaolin art. This is probably why the form is taught at an early stage. Knowing that the more you train in it, the more detail you will find.

Photo: Smashing a chopstick on the groin and the smashing of a plank of wood over the groin!

Not to be tried at home!

Relaxation

Relaxation is important when performing successful kung fu techniques. However, many see a relaxed body as a weakness and not, a strength! In the southern art the postures look strong and the body can seem tense. By training the combined tiger-crane art the practitioner incorporates the strength of the tiger and the softness and subtleness of the crane. Developing relaxation within the body and the limbs is a must for any kung fu student.

Not only is it important for your progress in martial arts. It is vital to relax in order to help you to cope with everyday life.

Only when you have learned to relax will your qi (chi) begin to flow. In order to relax the body first your mind must be relaxed and be calm. The levels of which you can learn to relax are like many skills. Each time you practice relaxation you can achieve a new level. Most people can learn to relax on the outside, it is however the inside which we need to learn how to relax.

The following is a simple relaxation exercise to practice with your partner.

Stand in a horse stance place both hands on your partner's shoulders and in turn push each other's shoulders trying to unbalance each other. Take it in turns and remember the posture and concentrate on rooting and relaxing.

Relaxation is best developed during your meditation sessions.

Candle training to help improve relaxation

This is a regular training exercise by many Shaolin schools and many hours can be spent punching out candles.

In order to improve relaxation in the arms try extinguishing a candle with a single punch. Do not touch the flame during the exercise. You may begin finishing your technique close to the candle in order to put out the flame but once you can repeat the exercise successfully you should move further away. You may choose to line up your candles in a row, say ten and once you can extinguish all the candles one after each other without failing it could be said that you have improved your relaxation. But do not stop here, as there are many other ways of improving your relaxation.

Both adults and children enjoy this exercise. But do ensure that children are well supervised throughout the training. The potential of someone hitting the candle is likely at some point. You are better to start well away from the candle and then move closer once the technique is correct. The punch should not be pulled back during the exercise. Therefore you cannot finish too close to the candle for obvious reasons.

Enjoy it!

Coin / pebble snatch

Another commonly used exercise is the coin or pebble snatch.

This is a popular exercise among many Shaolin groups. Often seen as a challenge to the student when their instructor offers the coin or pebble. The exercise was popularised during the 1970's *"Kung Fu "* series.

Get your partner to hold either a coin or pebble in the palm of their hand try to take it from them before they close their hand. You may at first start training with your hand above your partner's hand. Once you can take it from them on a regular basis try lowering your hands to the side of your body. Once you can do this exercise it means that you would probably be able to hit your partner before he had chance to block or move!

Improving relaxation

Relaxation should be treated as serious as any other part of the art. Learn to relax as a separate part of your training then you can concentrate fully on the task at hand.

Try to find a quiet spot where you are not going to get disturbed. The easiest way to relax is to lie down. Make yourself as comfortable as possible support the neck with a pillow.

Face upwards and place your hands at the side of your body.

Keep warm throughout the training.

Try to concentrate on relaxing the mind. When the mind is relaxed the easier it will become to relax the rest of your body. Once you have relaxed the mind relax the middle dan-tien and then your lower dan-tien. Breathe slowly and deeply each time you breath out you should feel the body relaxing further.
(Try breathing five or seven times during each exercise)

Once you have developed the relaxation in the body start trying to relax the rest of the body in turn. Start with the toes and feet then the ankles and calves. Continue working upwards to the knees thighs and hips. Again breathe in and out 5 or 7 times during each exercise.

Now begin relaxing the tips of your fingers, each finger joint, palm and backs of the hand working up in the same way as that of the leg begin relaxing the wrist, forearms elbows and upper arms.

Relax the shoulders then concentrate on relaxing the body once more.

Relax the neck and should you wish to continue to a more, deeper meditative state. Clear your mind by breathing in deeply and as you exhale clear all thoughts in the mind. Repeat the breathing as often as you wish.

Once you have completed your relaxation training take care to stretch slowly for a few moments.

Rooting

Many martial arts practitioners today fail to practice the basic stances and postures. Many believe that they are no longer an important part. Maybe this is because they have never been taught the correct posture etc. To miss out on the basics will weaken your entire art. The practice of each point is therefore vitally important.

Rooting is better achieved the more you learn to relax. Get the body structure right and your bone structure will support your relaxed body, therefore allowing the muscles to relax further. Once you have found this new level you can sink your qi downwards. Concentrate on feeling like water where you feel tension. Relax your mind and concentrate on relaxing that part of the body. You should visualize tension as say, an ice block. Put on the heater and watch it melt into water and then you will become more relaxed.

As mentioned earlier, when in the horse stance the most common way of developing the rooting of one's body is to visualize roots growing out of the feet like that of a tree. The root will become stronger as the tree grows. Likewise with practice the root of your stance will be stronger too.

Rooting will not only help make the techniques more powerful but will increase your stability and improve your balance when stepping, kicking etc.

If you think that you are now unable to move quickly from a deep-rooted stance. Think again!

The practice of "Tey Bey Sum Chien" will develop your shuffling skills. The more you train the faster you will get, but developing your root is most important.

The *Monkey* style of Shaolin kung fu will further improve your agility.

See stances and postures on further guidance that will help you improve your rooting.

Basic Meditation

It is often said that many illnesses start in the mind. Stress contributes to many people having time off work with headaches and migraines. Their mind is racing ahead. Worrying about how to do this or that.

If everyone started and finished their day with basic meditation, the next day would be easier to cope with. There are many ways in which to meditate and when we are training we should in fact be meditating.

Basic meditation may be practiced when sitting in what is known as lotus or half lotus position. It can of course be performed sitting, lying down, standing or even when moving. The spine should be kept straight and the body relaxed. The hands are normally placed on the top of the knees. Close your eyes and breathe slowly through the nose. If you do not wish to close your eyes then your focus should be downward so as not to be distracted by for example a picture or by something else in the room. Concentrate only on your breathing and allow thoughts that enter the mind to quickly disappear.

Practice at first for just five to ten minutes each day. Increase this time once you are comfortable with the posture. There is never a good or bad time to meditate. The important part is choosing when to practice. You should select a place and time during the day or evening when you can relax without disturbance. This then means the location and the environment you choose is equally important. Choose a comfortable and warm place where you feel safe. It would be unlikely for you to see someone practicing meditation in a noisy area.

We take time out to practice meditation so as to enable us to improve our meditation during our forms. When we are still we can concentrate more on our breathing than we do when we are training our forms. The mind wonders elsewhere on other aspects of the form; such as stances or techniques. When we are still we follow our breath more and we learn to control our qi.

A wonderful experience lies ahead for those who take time during their day to meditate. Breathe slowly and only when the breath is steady, the mind can relax. The bodies own energy is replenished during periods of meditation, making the tasks that lie ahead easier to deal with.

"Do not be a part of the universe, but become the universe"

"There will soon be no specific time for meditation, as you will eventually meditate all of the time"

Iron Shirt Qi-Gong
(Basic Exercises)

The training of the iron shirt is basically designed to develop the body's internal strength. After many years of such training the practitioner would be able to withstand powerful blows to their body, including their vital organs.

After the introduction of guns, many believed that they would not need to spend so much time developing their physical body in order to protect them. In today's world however it is fair to say that the practice of iron shirt may not save your life if confronted with such modern day weapons.

However, the desire to live healthier and longer, have always been the wish of many. Therefore the practice and development of the iron shirt qi gong is well worth the effort.

Iron shirt teaches you how to align the body structure so that *qi* (energy) can circulate and flow through the body. The *qi* that is then stored in the lower dan-tien can then be used to strengthen any part of the body the practitioner chooses.

Training of the iron shirt will help to develop the mind, body and spirit.

Above: A student takes an oath before being accepted to train in the "Shaolin inner-strength".

The combined use of the iron shirt training and kung fu training will therefore increase the student's ability to new levels never before deemed possible. It helps to develop the student physically and mentally.

The iron shirt training will help to develop the flow of qi and therefore increase the flow of blood and to help strengthen the muscles, tendons and bones.

The following exercises are merely a basic description of some of the iron shirt exercises trained in the Shaolin art. Such exercises are taught to dedicated, senior and initiated students only. The exact exercise is refined over a period time.

It is most important that you seek a qualified instructor before attempting the iron shirt training. In order to preserve the secret art of the iron shirt I have chosen to explain the exercises in a basic way only.

It is not advisable to practice iron shirt if you have high blood pressure or any heart problems. In the cases of women and the iron shirt training they should not practice the breathing and in particular the packing of the organs during a menstrual cycle and avoid completely when pregnant. You may however wish to practice some of the stances etc.

The reverse breathing would be used when training the iron shirt. It is normal however, for students to begin such exercises concentrating at first on the technique and correct form. Then later they would add the reverse breathing.

Exercises are refined over a period of time and unless you understand what to do seek a qualified instructor before you commence with your training.

Students would have to prove first their loyalty, dedication and respect for their teacher. It would be most unlikely that you would be taught the iron shirt exercises without completing at least eighteen months to two years of kung fu training.

Students wishing to train in the iron shirt would have to undergo an initiation with their teacher. It is however the teacher who selects the student and not the students who requests to be chosen.

There is no best time for a student to begin their training as all age groups have both advantages and disadvantages. It is not designed for the older person and students who have entered their mid forties *(not that this is old in kung fu terms)* with no physical training background may find the iron shirt training too strenuous and therefore should be avoided.

The following exercises are for reference only and should not be tried without supervision of a qualified instructor.

Iron Shirt Training Exercises

- ## Iron Shirt Exercise 1

'Holding the Heaven and Stabilising the Earth'

Stand with the feet shoulder width apart. Grasp the right wrist with the left hand and with the hands palm up in front of the lower dan tian. Throw the hands upwards over the head turning the palms to face the sky. Thus giving a stretch to the entire upper body and arms. Lower the hands to the start position in front of the dan tian and repeat 18 times in total. Rise up on to the toes at the end of each stretch upwards.

- ## Iron Shirt Exercise 2

'Open the window to look at the Moon'

Start as exercise 1 twist the body to face right drawing the right hand to the same side throw the hand over the head and outward to the left.
Repeat the exercise 18 times. Then change sides holding the left hand and repeat 18 times.

- **Iron Shirt Exercise 3**

'The Roc spreads its Wings'

Start with the left hand over the right, palms facing up in front of the dan tian. Lift both hands to shoulder height before twisting the palms to face downwards then throw both arms outwards and to the rear until the chest is stretched open. Keep the arms at least shoulder height. Rise up on to the toes as the arms are thrown back.
Repeat the exercise 18 times.

- **Iron Shirt Exercise 4**

'Carry the Tiger to the Hill'

Start as exercise 3. Squat down and as you stand up throw both hands upward and over the head turning the palms up to face the sky. Rise up on to the toes as you stretch up. Repeat 18 times.

- **Iron Shirt Exercise 5**

'The Green Dragon testing his claws'

Using the dragon claw position draw the hands inwards towards the chest palms facing in throw the hands out towards the rear at the left side. Repeat throwing to the right. Alternate from left to right side gripping the fingers at the end of each technique.
Repeat 36 times in total.

• Iron Shirt Exercise 6

'The Jade Lady Twisting Her Waist'

Starting from the forward facing position hands clenched turn to look over the left shoulder raising the right hand over the left side with both wrists facing each other. Look behind and towards the right heel. Repeat on the opposite side 18 times each side.

• Iron Shirt Exercise 7

'Brave Tiger Stretching his Back'

Face forwards using the tiger claw position bend forwards so that the back is horizontal with the ground. At the same time throw both hands forwards gripping at the end.
Repeat 18 times.

• Iron Shirt Exercise 8

'Twin Dragons go out to Sea'

From the start position with the hands in the dragon claw position both hands are raised above the head and after stretching upwards the hands are thrown out to both sides at the same time. Remain on toes as the hands are raised and thrown down to the sides.
Repeat 18 times.

- ### Iron Shirt Exercise 9

'Lohan Awakens'

From the start position fists closed squat down drawing both hands to the right side then throw out to the left side palms facing inwards. Repeat 18 times then change repeat 18 times to the opposite side.

- ### Iron Shirt Exercise 10

'The One Legged Kick'

Draw the heel upwards bending the leg and spring the foot forward and downward towards the ground.
Repeat 18 times each leg.

*Note this exercise should be the last exercise at the end of each iron shirt training session.

Basic Conditioning

Hands

While many people spend hundreds of pounds on equipment to build the body's strength, traditional methods, such as striking the gravel bag with the hand or fist would be normal for many Shaolin students. There is, of course, in today's world no real reason to develop an "iron hand" or "palm". The student today trains a more basic form of conditioning.

The hand is toughened enough so as to allow the student to break "house bricks" etc.

Using gravel bags and Chinese Medicine you need only spend a fraction of this amount. A gravel bag can be home made or if you wish not to spend time on such a task then it can be purchased for around five or six pounds. The Chinese medicine can be purchased for around twelve pounds for a 125ml bottle, which will last you for months.

Once you have your gravel bag you can choose to fill it with either sand or gravel. If you choose gravel then start striking the bag lightly to begin with until you become conditioned enough to increase the power of the strikes. Start slowly and increase the number of times you strike the bag using a different section of the hand. Some examples have been shown in next series of photographs.

It would be normal to start with about twenty strikes for each different part of the hand. Once this is comfortable increase in sets of ten. Like all kung fu training don't be in a hurry. Build up the number of strikes over twelve months. ie month one; ten strikes, month two; twenty strikes, month three; thirty strikes per each part of the hand and so on.

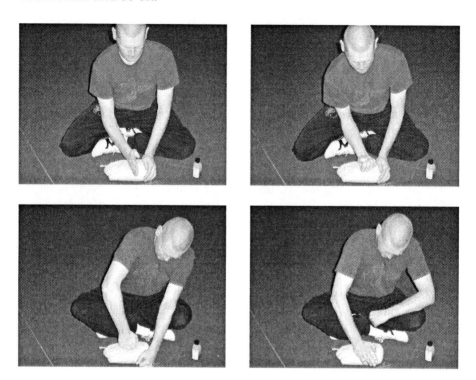

Warning: training beyond the basic levels may cause some nerve damage and cause even sterility. A well-conditioned hand that can break bricks etc may well be useful for self-defence but it should not be mistaken for an "iron hand" or "iron palm" this would result in the loss of finger nails and the hand would become blackened in its appearance.

You may also wish to condition the fingers.

Arms, Body & Legs

Similar to fist and hand conditioning striking the body is part of the daily shaolin training routine. Strikes to the various parts of the body would be part of the student's daily routine. Such areas would include the stomach, upper chest, side of the body, followed by striking of the legs and shins etc. The beginner should avoid striking the head.

Strike each point nine times in total. Similar to the fist conditioning, increase the number and the strength of your strike over a period of months not days.

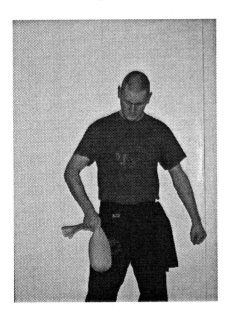 

Chinese Medicine
(Dit Dar Jau)

Make sure you use a good quality Chinese Medicine to prevent bruising when training. Most martial artists training the traditional styles would use *Dit Dar Jau* this is available from my own centre if you cannot find it elsewhere.

It is generally used for the treatment of bruises and muscle aches. It is for external use only. The Chinese masters were originally medical doctors, many of whom were practicing herbal medicine. They developed their own formulas and the ingredients where kept secret.

It is an essential part of the "iron palm" training of which involves striking hard objects with the hand. Generally used by rubbing a small amount into the area to be conditioned before and after the conditioning takes place. Avoid contact with eyes and open wounds and do not swallow. Read the instructions fully and as usual regarding any medicine store safely and keep out of reach of any children.

It was common in the old days for the medicine peddlers to set up their stall in a village to sell their herbal medicines. During such times many would perform amazing feats of strength such as bending spears on their throat or smashing bricks with their bare hands. This of course helped them to sell their medicine, before moving on to the next village. They are performed today at many Shaolin demonstrations to show the results of training Shaolin kung fu.

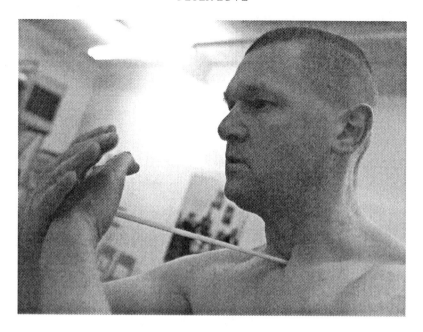

Above: Peter demonstrating the smashing of a chopstick on the throat.

In 2006 in front of a public audience Peter smashed 27 Chopsticks on the throat. The chopsticks were smashed individually over a one-minute period. Information gathered from various sources reveals that the world record was previously set at just 14.

TAI-CHI - The Lost Art

The Shaolin Soft Art –

The Shuang Yang Pei Ho Rou Ruan Chien

The following part of this book is dedicated to the Southern Shaolin soft art, which can easily be misinterpreted by many.

I have chosen to call this part of the book the lost art. Why? Because I feel that much of the modern tai chi is taught without real depth and has therefore lost some of the original teaching methods. The art from my experience has clearly been watered down by students copying what others appear to be doing and not learning the true ingredients of the original art!

Most people I believe now know what tai chi is. But very few understand how it should actually be taught. If you are unsure of its benefits then read any well being or medical article on stress related and many other illnesses and you will probably find a recommendation to practice tai chi. Imagine then if you could practice the shaolin soft art and benefit even more!

The Shaolin art has developed over the past one and half thousand years and in many cases much of the art has been lost. It is only through dedicated practice that the student can continue to develop.

One of the most under estimated styles of kung fu is that of tai chi and most people look upon tai chi as a dance which is practiced by only older people. Whilst the latter may be correct in many senses the Shaolin soft art passed down over the years hides a devastating secret art, that can only be taught and is not seen by the un-trained person.

If you are not getting a suitable workout and body toning then you are probably practicing a modern style. If you can find the original Shaolin soft art then you will notice the difference. Many of my students have practiced various styles of tai chi before training with myself. They all agree that our art offers much more in terms of physical development.

Although I must emphasize that each student works at their own pace, with no pressure on the physical aspect as long as they receive the right tuition, they all feel better after just a one-hour session.

De-stress is one of the key words. Many students come in from a hard days work therefore relaxation is a high priority when practicing the form.

Those who wish to develop a body that on the outside is soft, supple and flexible practice the White Crane form known as the "*Shuang Yang Pei Ho*". However, some thirty years later, on the inside it can be as hard as steel!

Once the student is familiar with each move of the form then the correct breathing can be added. It would be normal to practice the moves for up to eighteen month's of daily practice before including the breathing.

Like the iron shirt qi-gong, once the student is able to re-direct their qi, the student would concentrate on moving it to the point of concentration.

The Shuang Yang form also develops the technical skill of the student improving both balance and the ability to root their stance. Therefore it would be good practice for those involved in training hard external styles to train in the soft art in order to balance their training.

The learning of the Shuang Yang involves the student practicing the sixty-six moves. Each move is done slowly in as a gentle and soft way as possible. But at the end of each technique the student would feel rooted and firm. Once the move as been executed the student should feel relaxed and should be moving into the next step or technique.

Over a period of time the moves will become softer and the body will become more flexible with the flow of energy increasing. It will be natural for the student to feel warm energy at the point of their concentration.

The student before trying to practice the techniques of the form should first familiarize themselves with the stances. Practice the *horse* stance and the *bow and arrow* stance as previously descibed. Once you have trained and become familiar with these two stances practice stepping in both forward and backward direction. The steps should be soft and no sound should be heard when stepping. Each step should be practiced in order so as to perform each move continually from start to end.

ie Without stopping at different points during the step. At first this may prove difficult but with regular practice this can be achieved.

Once the student is familiar with the moves of the form they should develop the posture, which the body forms during the moves. These are similar to those of the iron shirt training methods. The spine bends both forward and backward starting at the base of the spine. The first thirteen moves of the form can help the student to develop these techniques and the student should develop and practice these moves until they are familiar with the changing body posture. Once you have trained this first section you will understand the rest of the moves more easily and will be able to apply the correct posture and breathing in order to maximize your training.

The student who trains this style in the way that it was originally taught will develop a stronger and healthier body.

In general and simple terms when you step and lift the root you should breathe in and when you sink into your stance you should breathe out. Remember that at first practice the moves before trying to co-ordinate them with the posture and breathing.

The "Shuang Yang Pei Ho Rou Ruan Chien" roughly translates to "Frost and Sun White Crane Soft and Gentle Art". Reading into the words of the form suggests that this is not just a soft form. But suggests that there is something strong and powerful. The mere suggestion of the word "Sun" alone should tell you that the form is strong and powerful.

Basic Footwork

The following footwork should be applied during the training of the form.

In general the front foot opens before you lift the root of the back foot. The opposite is performed when stepping back. That is the step is made backwards while the front foot is still rooted and when the back foot is then rooted the front foot turns in.

Directions

Directions; Forward - North, Backwards - South, Right - East and Left - West. Other directions will include North West, North East, South West and South East.

The directions are given to simplify and explain to the student the direction of each step or move. In most practices of qi-gong it is normal to begin facing the sun.

The sixty-six moves from the form

1. *Opening salute to the sun.*

Start by facing north. Stand in a relaxed horse stance.

Step forward with the right leg, into a bow and arrow stance. The hands come up from the left side and across the body to form an outer block with the wrist. The fingertips should be at eye level palms facing in. The wrists then turn to face forwards and the elbows sink. As the spine folds, the fingertips should lower to shoulder height.

2. *The cross.*

Drawing the hands in as you step back with the right foot into the horse stance facing east. The left hand, nearest the body, with the hands in such a position as if you were carrying a ball, pressed against the chest. Do not bring the hands to close to the chest. The body turns to face to the right side and the elbows are kept down as the hands are drawn in to the shoulders at which point the hands are pushed out to either side. The fingers should face upwards with the palms facing out to either side at shoulder height.

3. The general carrying his seal.

Grip the right hand to form a fist and lower to the side of the body, just below the ribs. At the same time open the left foot and then step forward in a northerly direction back into the bow and arrow stance. The right fist executes a straight punch; while the left hand is drawn into a defensive position, in front of the sternum and next to the right elbow, palm facing the elbow. The fingers of the left hand should face upwards.

4. Two shoulders going downwards.

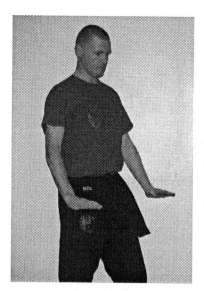

Repeat as move two but when the hands have reached the shoulders both hands push downwards to either side of the body in a slightly forward position. The fingertips should face forward therefore giving a stretch to each wrist.

5. The golden scissors.

Step forward to a northerly direction into the right foot bow and arrow stance the hands are drawn into the waist as the step is being made and then both hands move forwards with the palms facing up. The right hand crosses over the left hand and when almost fully extended forward both hands turn over so that the palms face down.

6. The beginning of heaven and earth.

 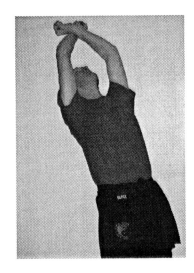

Stepping forward into left bow and arrow stance the hands are gripped and then move upwards and over the head. The body is carefully stretched backwards and the hands are moved in a circular motion back towards the front.

The body at which point as returned to an upright position with the spine stretched in a forward bent position and the elbows are now drawn inwards.

7. The hungry tiger grasping a goat.

Stepping forward into the right bow and arrow stance and by raising the chest and straightening the spine the body posture will in turn lift both elbows upwards and therefore both hands raise to about eyebrow level.

8. *The old tree shaking its roots.*

Once the hands have reached eye level, remaining in the same stance both hands open, fingers facing upwards and the palms towards you. Moving the hands from left to right execute a low right open hand block. The fingers should face down and forward. The left hand finishes against the right elbow, with the fingers facing upwards.

9. *The golden cockerel standing on one leg.*

Open the right foot and draw the left foot forward in a circular sweeping motion bringing the left foot slightly under the right knee so as to form the crane stance. During the foot movement the hands circle and the right hand finishes at the side of the body palms facing in, fingers facing down. The left hand finishes at the centre of the body with the palm facing to the right and the fingertips facing upwards.

10. The leap.

Leaping upwards, change to a left crane stance.

11. The Immortal casting his net.

Step forward into the right bow and arrow stance. The hands make the same movement as the first move *the salute to the sun* but instead of sinking downwards the hands are pushed forward palms facing down. The left hand once again traces the movement of the right elbow.

12. The sage god appoints a scholar.

After closing the right fist pull the right foot back into a right foot forward cat stance at the same time drawing the right fist back to the waist. The left hand lowers inwards parallel with floor as the right hand makes an uppercut technique.

13. *The iron hammer sinking into the river.*

Step forward into the right bow and arrow stance. The right hand drops in a pendulum like action and strikes to the groin. The left hand again traces the movement of the right elbow finishing in front of the sternum.

The above moves should be practiced daily until you are familiar with each of the moves.

Practicing to relax the body as much as possible during your training. Once you have become familiar with the moves move on to the next few moves. Build the form slowly.

14. *Double turns of the cross.*

Drawing the hands in as you step back, with the right foot to face east into the horse stance. With the left hand nearest the body, and the hands in such a position, that as if you were carrying a ball pressed against the chest. The body turns to face to an easterly direction and the elbows are kept down as the hands are drawn in to the shoulders, at which point the hands are pushed out to either side. The fingers should face upwards with the palms facing out to either side. Then step back with the left foot to face west repeat the move with the body facing to the west. This is the same movement as the second move with second stance facing the opposite direction.

15. Ringing the bell and beating the drum.

Clench both hands, open the right foot, step forward into a left bow and arrow stance facing north the arms are rotated so that the left arm comes over to the right side before dropping into a low left block. The arms are kept in line with each other until the block is made then the right hand drops to the font position as the left hand is drawn back up to the front to the same level as the right. This final move would be used to break an opponents arm.

To help with this move use a six-foot staff and rest it behind the shoulders and stretch both hands out to either end. Rotate the staff in circular direction. To avoid any injury to the neck ensure that the staff is not pressed against the back of the neck.

16. Salute to the sun.

Open the left foot and step forward into a right bow and arrow stance and repeat the first move of the form, *salute to the sun.*

17. The turning of the cross.

Step back with the right foot into the horse stance facing the east immediately open the right foot and step forward into another horse stance facing west. Drawing the hands in as you step back into the horse stance. The left hand nearest the body, and the hands in such a position, that as if you were carrying a ball pressed against the chest. The hands are pushed out to either side. The fingers should face upwards with the palms facing out to either side.

18. The golden scissors.

Open the left foot so as to face outwards and step in a forty-five degree angle to face in a southeast direction into a bow and arrow stance. The hands are drawn into the waist as the step is being made and then both hands move forwards with the palms facing up. The right hand crosses over the left hand and both arms extend to a forward position.

19. Parting the grass to find the snake.

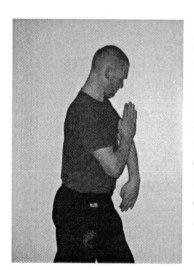

Step across with the right foot turning the body 180 degree's so as to face in the opposite direction ie North West. The left hand makes a lower block and the right hand traces the left elbow. There are a number of versions on how to execute this move and the move can include repeating the move on the opposite side before finishing back in the above position.

- *The following moves should continue in a straight line in a North West direction.*

20. *Two butterflies flying together.*

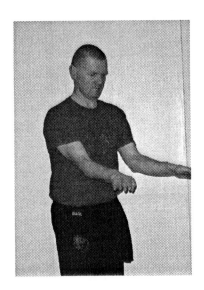 

Continue facing North West step forward into a right bow and arrow stance and make a double inward high-level open hand block leading into a double open hand lower crane block. Turn the wrists, first outwards and then inwards towards the body and make a double forward strike with the fingertips to the shoulder height, palms facing inwards.

21. *Parting the clouds to see the moon.*

Step forward making a left hand high roof block followed by an upper crane block. The right hand is pulled back to the waist in the open hand position.

22. The firework shooting into to sky.

The left hand lowers inwards parallel with floor as the right hand is closed before making an uppercut technique.

23. The sage grinding the rice mill.

Step out in an easterly direction with the right foot. The right clenched fist lowers and faces the left palm. Circle both hands so as to perform an elbow strike to the right before facing back into a northwest direction. At which point the left hand performs a high-level roof block with the palm protecting the right temple and the right fist executes a straight punch in the direction of travel.

24. 100 birds returning to their nest.

Used generally as a wristlock or similar action. Step forward with the right foot into bow and arrow stance. Drop the left hand onto the right palm. Both hands then circle in a clockwise direction, sweeping first inwardly at low level then into an outward upper block to the right. The left hand remains in contact with the right hand throughout the movement.

25. The mandarin duck searching for its nest.

The above move is repeated twice more stepping forward first into a left bow and arrow stance then forward into a right bow and arrow stance.

26. The ferocious tiger returning to the mountains.

Again depending on the student's ability this move can be done in various ways. I will explain only the basic move and application so that you can understand the technique.

Step with the left foot turning almost 180 degrees facing in a south direction. The right hand performs and inward high level block before sweeping into a

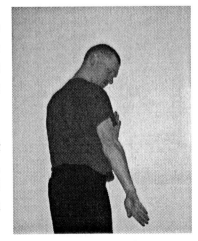

groin strike in a northwest direction. The left palm should return to the centre with the palm facing to the right and the fingers facing upwards.

- *The following moves should be performed in South East direction.*

27. *The white horse sheds it saddle.*

Stepping with the right foot into an easterly direction. The right hand sweeps around into the northwest direction and for an example grabs hold of the groin of the opponent. The left hand then strikes with the blade of the hand while the right hand pulls away. The left hand finishes with the palm facing downward and the right palm finishes facing upwards. The shoulder is kept sunk and the elbow in, the wrist is pushed outward and fingertips face inward.

28. *The white horse sheds it saddle.*

Repeat the above move with opposite hands after first stepping in a south direction with the left foot into a bow and arrow stance. The left hand now grabs the groin before the right hand strikes.

The above moves have more than one application and could be adapted so as to perform a takedown technique.

29. *The whirling golden scissors.*

Step into a left foot bow and arrow stance facing a south east direction both hands sweep inwards to perform an inward double upper open hand block before dropping into and outward double open hand lower crane block. Both hands continue to circle into the waist before striking forward with both palms facing upwards.

- *The following moves are the same as the above but moves 30 to 37 should be done in a north east direction and moves 38 and 39 in a south west direction.*

    - *Repeat moves 18 to 28.*

30. *Parting the grass to find the snake.*

Pivot on the heels turning the body 90 degree's so as to face a North East direction. As move 18, the left hand makes a lower block and the right hand traces the left elbow. There are a number of versions on how to execute this move and the move can include repeating the move on the opposite side before finishing back in the above position.

31. *Two butterflies flying together.*

Continue facing North East step forward into a right bow and arrow stance and make a double inward high-level block leading into a double lower crane block. Turn the wrists, first outwards and then inwards towards the body and make a double forward strike with the fingertips to the shoulder height, palms facing inwards.

32. Parting the clouds to see the moon.

Step forward making a left hand high roof block followed by an upper crane block. The right hand is pulled back to the waist.

33. The firework shooting into the sky.

The left hand lowers inwards parallel with floor as the right hand makes an uppercut technique.

34. The sage grinding the rice mill.

Step out in a south direction with the right foot. The right clenched fist lowers and faces the left palm. Circle both hands so as to perform an elbow strike to the right before facing back into a northeast direction. At which point the left hand performs a high-level roof block with the palm protecting the right temple and the right fist executes a straight punch in the direction of travel.

35. 100 birds returning to their nest.

Step forward with the right foot into bow and arrow stance. Drop the left hand onto the right palm. Both hands then circle in a clockwise direction, sweeping first inwardly at low level then into an outward upper block to the right side. The left hand remains in contact with the right hand throughout the movement.

36. *The mandarin duck searching for its nest.*

The above move is repeated twice more stepping forward first into a left bow and arrow stance then forward into a right bow and arrow stance.

37. *The ferocious tiger returning to the mountains.*

Step with the left foot turning almost 180 degrees facing a westerly direction.

The right performs and inward high level block before sweeping into a groin strike in a northwest direction. The left palm should return to the centre with the palm facing to the right and the fingers facing upwards.

38. *The white horse sheds its saddle.*

Stepping with the right foot into a south direction. The right hand sweeps around into the northeast direction and for an example grabs hold of the groin of the opponent. The left hand then strikes with the blade of the hand while the right hand is drawn back into the position shown. The left hand finishes with the palm facing downward and the right palm finishes facing upwards.

39. *The white horse sheds its saddle.*

Repeat the above move with opposite hands after first stepping in a west direction with the left foot into a bow and arrow stance. The left hand now grabs the groin before the right hand strikes.

- *The form continues with:*

40. *The sweep of arm and leg.*

There is no repeat of the golden scissors movement after the second white horse sheds the saddle. The form continues with the sweep of the arm and leg. Spinning in an anti clockwise direction on the left foot the right foot sweeps around until the body is facing back to the north: The right foot is drawn inwards to finish with the sole of the foot slightly below the left knee. At the same time the hands are drawn into a cross position with the left hand nearest the body. Both palms face outward to the sides and the fingers should point upwards.

Step back with the right foot and draw the left knee and left elbow together so that the body is facing east standing on the right leg. Then step forward with the left foot so as to face north in a deep bow and arrow stance sweeping the left hand downwards and forwards.

41. *The lazy tiger stretching his back.*

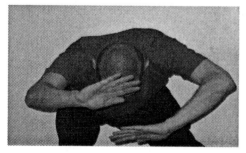 Step forward with the right foot again into a deep and low bow and arrow stance slowly circle the hands with the palms facing away from the body. With each circle the body should lower

further forward and the hands stretch further away from the body. The spine is stretched and twisted in a snake like action.

42. *Two swallows diving together.*

  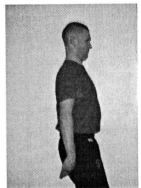

After stretching out into the lazy tiger position open the left foot slightly and step up with the right foot so as to face west. Step with the right foot behind and across the left foot pushing the right knee behind the left knee. As the feet cross the hands should draw up and cross each other in an inward direction. Step out with the left foot into a horse stance drop the hands into a double lower crane block before lowering the hands to the side of the body with the palms facing behind and the fingers facing downwards. This move is then repeated once more in the same direction.

43. *Both legs come together.*

Step up with the left foot so as to face north both feet together drawing both hands into a cross position.

44. Consecutive kicks.

Once in the cross position with the knees slightly bent. Slowly raise the left knee before extending the foot forward into a heel kick position. The kick should be performed slowly with the supporting leg in a slightly bent position. Extend both hands forward with the palms facing down the left hand slightly lower than the right. Execute a right circling kick of which the instep touches first the left palm then continues to touch the right palm before the leg bends and then lowering slowly into a right bow and arrow stance still facing north.

45. Two dragons rushing out of the sea.

Both hands sink towards the ground palms facing downwards. Then lift both hands together drawing them towards the shoulders before pushing forward with both palms facing forward and the fingertips facing up.

46. Opening the lock on the wall.

Still facing north, step forward into a left bow and arrow stance. Both hands cross in the center of the body with the right traveling upward towards the left side and the left hand traveling downwards to the right side as the elbows meet close both hands before opening the hands in to its final position.

47. The scattering of petals

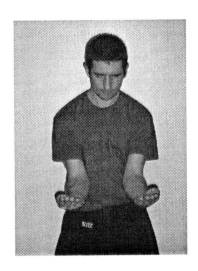

Step forward into a right bow and arrow stance. Lowering both hands forward and from the lower dan tian level raise both hands upwards.

On reaching eye level the hands open and continue circling over the head before lowering to each side of the body and striking forward to the soft points of the body.

48. *The tyrant stretching his bow.*

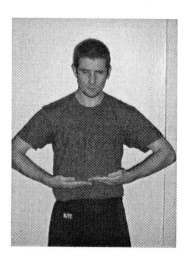 

Step up feet together draw the hands upward with the palms facing up and the fingers pointing together. On reaching shoulder height turn the palms to face down and pull the shoulders back so as to stretch the chest open. Lower both hands to the cross position.

49. The lion cub opening his mouth.

Step out with the right foot lowering the right hand to the side of the body. Step out with the left foot in a 45 degree angle in a northeast direction and execute a left hand palm strike (fingertips facing up) and a right hand palm strike (fingers facing to the right side palm up).

50. The lion cub opening his mouth.

Step back with the left foot into its previous position lowering the left hand to left side of the body and the right hand to the center of the body. Step forward with the right foot into bow and arrow stance facing a north direction and execute the double palm strikes. The left fingers facing to the left side palm facing up and the right hand finger tips facing up.

51. *The roc spreading its wings.*

Step back with the right foot into a horse stance facing east, drawing the hands in as you step back. The left hand, nearest the body with the hands in such a position, that as if you were carrying a ball, pressed against the chest. The body turns to face to the right side and the elbows are kept down as the hands are drawn into the shoulders at which point the hands are pushed out to either side. The fingers should face downwards with the palms facing forward at shoulder height.

52. *The Immortal pointing the way.*

Step forward into a right bow and arrow stance facing north lower both hands to the side of the body. Strike with both hands in a forward direction to your own shoulder height at the end of the technique the hands twist inward to face downward.

53. *Two swallows spitting.*

Step forward into a left bow and arrow stance.

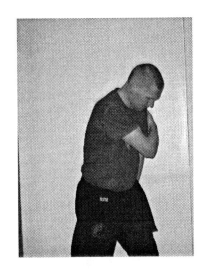

At the same time the left hand palm strikes the right arm and the back of the right hand strikes the left kidney area. The hands then swap positions. That is, the right hand strikes the left arm and the left hand strikes the right kidney area.

Both hands are then lowered in front of the body before rising upwards in to a double wrist strike.

54. The poisonous snake grasping the throat.

Step forward into a right stance and execute a salute to the sun movement. At the end of the move shuffle forwards and close the hands as if grasping the throat with the right hand.

55. The white crane reaching for the sky.

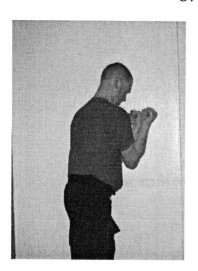 

Turn the body to face a west direction. The elbows are drawn inwards. The right leg sweeps across the front leg and then the left leg sweeps behind the right leg both feet travel in a south direction and finish on the same line in which they started. The move is a jumping leap finishing with both fists sinking towards the ground. The stance is much longer in order to drop the body in a lower position.

56. The boatman rowing the boat.

From the above position both arm arms rotate in a clockwise direction. That is starting from the low closed fist position. Open both hands and circle from low to front to high to back and from back to low returning you to the start position.

57. The little devil pushing the boat.

Once you have completed the boatman rowing the boat the feet and body should face back to the north position and the hands are drawn in a sweeping action forward at the same time the body weight shifts from the left leg to the right finishing in a deep low forward right stance.

58. The lotus flower sprinkling water.

Bring the left foot forward in a sweeping motion to the front before bringing it back to finish feet together. At the same time circle both hands inwards parallel with the floor and forwards at chest height until the wrists cross. The fingers should individually form a wave like action during this move.

59. Returning to the cross.

The right hand crosses over the left hand followed by the left hand twisting first inwards towards the body before both hands twist so that the palms are facing outwards and the fingertips pointing upwards.

60. The wind sweeping the willow leaves.

Step back into a low horse stance facing east.

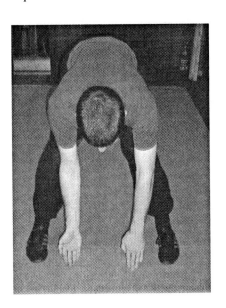 

Both arms extend downwards with the right palm facing outwards and the left palm facing inwards.

In a clockwise direction circle the arms when reaching the high level change the direction of each hand so as to finish at a low level position with the left palm facing outwards and the right palm inwards and with the fingers pointing towards the ground. Bend the legs during the exercise so as to sink low into the stance. There are times when you need not bend forward but sink into the low horse stance instead. This would of course depend on its application. You may also wish to bend the spine backwards as the hands come over the head. Make sure you are firmly in your stance before bending forward or backward.

61. The wind sweeping the willow leaves.

Repeat the above move in the opposite direction by stepping back into a low horse stance, facing west.

Both arms extend downwards with the left palm facing outwards and the right palm facing inwards. In an anti clockwise direction circle the arms when reaching the high level change the direction of each hand so as to finish at a low level position with the right palm facing outwards and the left palm inwards and with the fingers pointing towards the ground.

62. *The beauty looking in the mirror.*

Step forward with the left foot into a bow and arrow stance. From your original low position bring the body upwards and at the same time the right hand performs a high roof block and the left hand strikes with the fingertips.

63. *The final salute to the sun.*

Repeat the first move of the form by stepping forward with the right leg, into a bow and arrow stance. The hands come up from the left side and across the body to form an outer block. The fingertips should be at eye level palms facing in. The wrists then turn to face forwards and the elbows sink. The fingertips should lower to shoulder height.

64. *The parting cross.*

Repeat the second move of the form by drawing the hands in as you step back with the right foot into the horse stance facing east. The left hand nearest the body with the hands in such a position, as if you were carrying a ball pressed against the chest. The body turns to face to the right side and the elbows are kept down as the hands are drawn in to the shoulders at which point the hands are pushed out to either side. The fingers should face upwards with the palms facing out to either side at shoulder height.

65. *The child carrying the shield.*

Step forward facing north into a right bow and arrow stance. The right hand sweeps across the body from right to left with the palm facing the body before turning the palm outwards and sweeping from left to right finishing in front of the centre line. While the right hand makes the low sweep the left traces the right elbow before finishing in front of the sternum palm facing to the right and the fingers facing upwards.

66. *Both shoulders sinking to the ground.*

Repeat as move four. By stepping back into a horse stance facing east. When the hands have reached the shoulders both hands push downwards to either side of the body in a slightly forward position. The fingertips should face forward therefore giving a stretch to each wrist.

Although this is the last move the direction finished is to the east. You may either choose to finish facing this direction or if, for example, you were showing the form at an exhibition you might finish in away so that you are facing forward in the direction from which you originally started the form.

Should you wish to understand and develop the Shuang Yang Pei Ho form you must practice regularly and you should try to find an instructor who would be willing to teach you.

Further Shuang Yang Pei Ho Training

Congratulations you have now finished the Shuang Yang Pei Ho Form. But remember this is a guide to the basic steps only.

Do not however be in a hurry to learn something else. As you have only been given the first sixty-six building blocks to practice. That is you only have the basic A-Z moves. You have a lifetime of practice ahead of you and each time you practice you will no doubt at first forget some of the moves or do them in the wrong order. That's all right, just repeat it again and again until you remember the form.

If you look at the form move by move and refer to each as a single building block. When first practicing it is a bit like watching robots. They move from A to Z but forget to pass through B, C, D and E etc.

So now building block one becomes split into four new blocks in order to improve simply the hand techniques. Now lets divide the block again into eight pieces and look closely at the footwork. That is opening the foot, the transfer of weight, lifting the root, stepping and rooting the foot again.

Many students and even teachers overlook the basics and therefore have nothing more to learn. Now instead of just one block we have eight for only our first move.

Just when you thought it was going well! I am now going to split the block further. How may you ask can a simple move be divided into even more blocks? Well let us look at training the body to relax and flow. Let us take a look at the changing posture during the movements and let us look at our breathing. How many of your moves are external and many are internal? Every move should begin from the lower dan-tian.

Now I have hopefully encouraged you to break down what you are practicing and in the long term improve on what you may be already doing. Our single building block as now multiplied several times and if you wish to multiply it further try looking at the many other ingredients of the art! .... Like co-ordination, concentration and the applications etc. After about three years or so of daily practice you will understand the form much more. However remember that the many blocks that you now have should be fused into one complete move! Eventually you can empty the mind and practice the form as part of your meditation practice. But before you can do this you must break it down.

Now we have something new to practice and develop every day.

The form after up to thirty years of regular practice would produce a strong and healthy body through the correct training methods. This is because it is closely related to the iron shirt training. Sadly, like much of the kung fu it has been lost over years. Much of the modern tai chi will miss out the stretching and firmness created through out the body. Note I said firmness and not tension. Tension is solid / hard and slow to move. While firmness allows you to remain relaxed and therefore enable you to move swiftly and smoothly.

There are many paths to our goal of achieving perfection of the form. The practice of the basics should be ongoing through our training. When you see your teacher do what you consider to be an advanced move. Ask him what is he is actually practicing? The answer should be the basics!

The Chinese Lion & Dragon

Students performing a traditional part of the Chinese culture and Kung Fu.
The lion dance. Good Lion Dancers are normally good kung fu students.

A Chinese Dragon Team performing in Singapore.

The skills required to perform both the lion and dragon dance require lots of dedicated practice.

Finding the Shaolin Way

Over the past 36 years I personally have trained over 100 different types of forms or *katas*. Knowing lots of forms however impressive they may look to a student is not important. What are important are the ingredients of the forms you train.

Do not expect to learn these ingredients overnight. They are passed on to only a few disciples. In order to study you will of course expect to pay for your training. This does not however give you the right to learn the ingredients or elements of kung fu. You will be expected to earn these elements.

To personally show my own commitment to learning I travelled to Singapore to meet and train with a Shaolin master. My spirit, mind and body where all tested during my stay. Just the living conditions alone would have put off many. There where no western toilet facilities in the place where I stayed. There was neither a bed nor any hot water. Instead I lay and slept on a mattress and took cold showers twice a day. Once I had been shown where the local (MRT) transport station was I travelled alone for many journeys around the island. On one occasion while settling down for the evening I remember noticing that several of the oranges had fallen from the altar where I was staying. I picked them up and placed them back on the altar so that they would not role off again. During a period of relaxation in the late evening I noticed what I thought was a local cat pass by my room. A second closer look revealed it was in fact a rat. I lost sight of the rat and thought nothing more about it until the next day. As I was leaving I noticed the oranges on the floor once again! A close inspection revealed that they had become the rat's supper!

I do not wish to complain about the hospitality during my stay in Singapore. I am merely pointing out to those of you who wish to study and learn Shaolin way you must first look at yourself. Remove any self-ego that you may have. Stop wanting and you will eventually find what you are looking for.

Such experiences during my stay in Singapore taught me to respect what I had back home. But at the same time it taught me to no longer want anything material. I could survive on small simple meals and drinks and since my return home I have concentrated on further developing my mind, body and spirit. I no longer care or require about having this or that thing. My life is now dedicated to learning the Shaolin way and is much richer for it, even though I now own much less than I did say twenty years ago.

Although many a Shaolin student or disciple, may live and train in a Shaolin Temple. It does not mean that you cannot begin your journey outside of the temple. Start now and see where you finish.

Etiquette

Respect – Brotherhood - Diligence

Wherever you choose to train your martial arts etiquette will pay an important part. Whatever martial art you study you will come across similar rules and codes of conduct to follow.

You will almost certainly be expected to bow on entry and leaving your place of training. Bowing to your instructor at the beginning and the end of your training will be a certain requirement at any centre. You will be expected to remove any outdoor footwear before stepping on to a training area. Everyone should observe the code of conduct, at all times.

When you join a martial arts group you will almost certainly see a code of conduct and set of rules that you should follow during your training.

The Shaolin art first and foremost will try to create harmony amongst its members and therefore the term Brotherhood will be mentioned. This will involve treating everyone as if they were your own family.

Respecting each other and in particular your seniors and instructors is of great importance. If you show little respect to your instructor for example you will probably find that he will not teach you the way he would have normally. Should you show no signs of respect the chances are you will not be allowed to continue your training.

You will be asked to follow reasonable instructions by your teacher. You must be honest at all times and never bully anyone.

Responsibility means what it says. You should not for example use any of the skills taught to you outside unless in extreme danger.

You should at all times train diligently in order to pursue your art.

Many clubs will have such Codes of Conduct and a set of rules, which you should follow. In particular you should not drink alcohol or use any drugs other than those prescribed by a doctor.

Disciples and Students

In order to learn you must first become a student. Listen to the instructions given by the teacher. It is not about how much you do but how well you do it. What do you do when the class as finished? Do you leave immediately or do you take time out to check that all the equipment is put back correctly? Or do you leave it all to the teacher? To learn more you should help with the chores, like cleaning the training room or other areas. Make tea and wash the dishes. Ensure you are polite at all times and the teacher will want to teach you more. Do not be false with your help. He will know if you did it for the right reason or not. Do not expect him to teach you because you made one cup of tea on your first day. Try doing it for six months. Most importantly commit to your training and give 100% all of the time.

After four years or so you should be well into your training. Try to avoid asking too many questions on what and why you are doing a certain movement or exercise but practice what you are told not what you want to do. Avoid copying others who may be in the room at the same time. They are probably training a more advanced part of the art and if you try to copy you will certainly get it wrong.

To become a disciple you must show a good understanding of the martial art. You must be trustworthy loyal to your teacher, have a good knowledge of the art you are studying be mature and sincerely dedicated. A disciple is someone who has chosen to follow the way of their leader.

A disciple would be expected to perform chores and tasks without question.

It is unlikely that you will become a disciple under the age of twenty-five. You need to first know yourself and be sure in the direction you wish to travel. In today's more commercial world people are not likely to give up what they already may have and what they still want materially very easily. That is why you will not see to many young disciples. There life is full of distractions and therefore unable to concentrate on achieving the Shaolin way of life.

Although some students may begin their iron shirt training after only eighteen months to two years of membership. It does not mean that they have become a disciple to the teacher. This is just a further test to see which student will develop the elements of a disciple.

After about ten to fifteen years you can expect to be quite an expert in your chosen style. But you will find that now you are able to learn even more from your teacher. During your ten to fifteen years of practice remember though that your teacher too has been practicing and developing his skills!

At eighteen I was winning tournaments and in fact began teaching at only fourteen. Do you think I am teaching what I learned over thirty years ago?

Definitely not, I have searched for new skills to build on the ones that I had already acquired and time as taught me much more.

In ten years time I will teach the new or refined skills I have acquired!

The colour of your sash is unimportant in Shaolin kung fu training. You did not train to earn this coloured sash and that coloured sash. You joined to begin a new way of life. Most groups studying Shaolin kung fu do not have different colour sashes to distinguish a student's rank. Our particular group uses the black coloured sash for all students. It is used for training purposes only and not for the level attained.

After all we are a brotherhood and are therefore, all equal. You will know who your teacher is and therefore he will not need to show his superiority with the colour of his sash. If clubs choose to have different colour sashes, then this is their personal choice. Time changes everything. Let us not worry about minor things. I have often thought and even my students have asked why we don't have different colour sashes. This is a debate that will continue to run forever. For example if a beginner wears a white sash an intermediate student wears blue and an advanced student wears purple, a disciple wears orange and a master wears black. What then when a student feels he has practiced more and is better than a same ranking student? Does he need a different colour? What about the mature student who as dedicated thirty years or more but is not as physically fit as a younger student. Does he need to wear a different colour? There will always be some for and some against the idea of coloured sashes. When the time is right, then I may change our system.

The three tools you require to learn kung fu:

One you will need to find:
He will be your teacher.

The other two you already have!
They are your eyes and ears.

Final comment

I hope that now you have read this book that you are eager to learn more about Shaolin kung fu. If you have enjoyed reading it then please tell others.

Remember that copying from a video or learning from a book, including this one, will not teach you the entire art!

Go, seek and find your teacher.

Good Luck with your training.

Respect to the Brotherhood.

Notes

For more details of classes or courses run by the F.M.A.
please write to:

F.M.A.
First Floor, Archway Garage
Uttoxeter Road
Longton
Stoke-on-Trent
Staffordshire
ST3 1PF

Or visit www.fma-shaolin.co.uk

The F.M.A. Founded 1999

Printed in the United Kingdom
by Lightning Source UK Ltd.
118511UK00001B/307-336